# Halloween
## Life of the Party

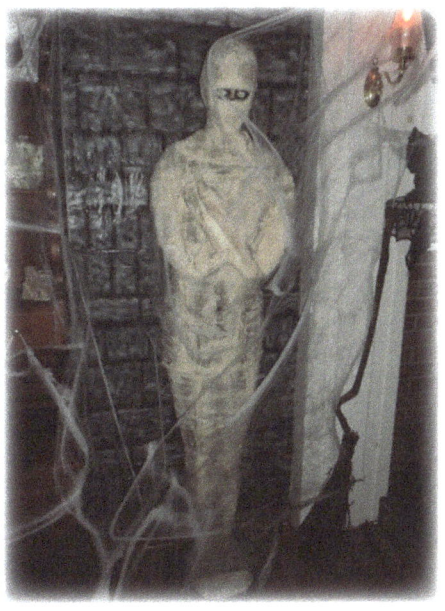

A unique compilation of wickedly creative ideas for throwing an authentic Halloween costume party featuring prop selection, best use of available space, special effects/illusions, music, games, prizes, food/drink, invitations... everything to drive the "life" of the party!

## Dick Durland
### Photos by Sue Durland

NEWMAN SPRINGS PUBLISHING
320 Broad Street
Red Bank, NJ 07701

First originally published by Newman Springs Publishing 2020

ISBN 978-1-64801-192-4 (Paperback)
ISBN 978-1-64801-193-1 (Digital)

Printed in the United States of America

To Sue

# Contents

# Preface

OCD. My wife says I suffer from it. Knowing that if you leave me alone at my work desk long enough the items that appear there will eventually, mysteriously form right angles with each other is proof enough for me, but I believe "suffer" is not the proper term as I hardly ever realize I am doing "it." Obsessive-Compulsive Disorder. Sounds like a deficiency, but I can't say that I fully agree because when properly channeled, this same "disorder" can be of great value. Because of it, whenever I apply myself to any given task and before my name officially goes on it, somewhat lofty expectations must be met. All right, obsessive compulsive...THAT much I agree with.

* * * * *

One day, my wife suggests we attempt throwing a Halloween party. I'm all in...perhaps to a fault. And that's the point. She knows once I've accepted a challenge, it's like leaving me alone with an untidy desktop. I may not consciously be aware of it, but I immediately go about the business of obsessing until I'm either satisfied enough for my stamp of approval to officially go on it, or I run out of time. As it turns out (at least where our Halloween party is concerned), I run out of time...every year. But by starting over again right where I left off year after year, I've continued to channel my "disorder" into creating the consummate Halloween event, making it ever more deserving of "my name."

And so it goes. I admit that it's overkill, still two things remain true. We show our invited guests the best possible time we can, and along the way, I've discovered a lot about the inner workings of throwing as authentic a Halloween party as you're ever going to come across. On top of identifying the major components such as backdrop, props, sound effects, games, music, etc. through trial and error, I've developed the detail, special effects, illusions, and assorted minutia (some store bought, some homemade) that best compliment a living, breathing, state-of-the-art Halloween costume party.

For your amusement, contained in the following pages is the culmination of all my time-tested ideas, discoveries, and creations toward perfecting the ultimate Halloween bash. Collectively, they comprise... *the life of the party!*

# Making Halloween an Event

We do not stop playing because we are old. We
grow old because we stop playing.

—Benjamin Franklin

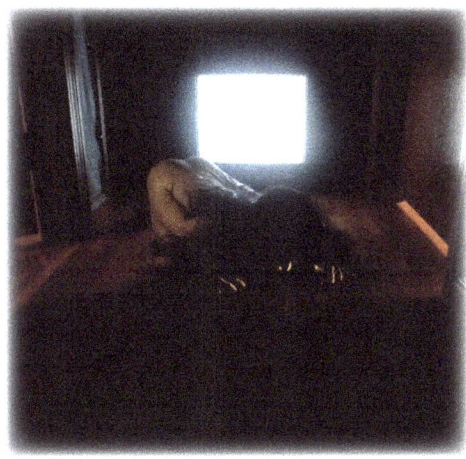

We've held our Halloween party six out of the last seven years...watching it
become ever more elaborate with each iteration by continually adding detail
into every production. It's more a labor of love than anything else as everyone who attends "forces" us to throw the party over and over. The resulting
transformation of our home occurs over a several day period with the first
number of hours being spent on the wallpaper alone as the entire first floor
becomes completely "dungeon-ized," flame pots, and all. Two sound systems
play simultaneously, one banging out the best of eighties hard rock, the other
an uninterrupted thunder/lightning storm. I include the "lightning" part

9

since we cleverly conceal a foot pedal under a love seat by the back door that runs outside to a series of floodlights mounted on posts strategically placed around the back of the house to create the actual "lightning." But I digress. Before I get ahead of myself, let me take a deep breath and start at the beginning.

Our philosophy: Create the proper environment, and THEY'LL bring the party! And when it comes to throwing a Halloween party, props and decor play a big role toward upping the entertainment value. So it's particularly important to make the most of your available space in order to produce the kind of setting that will increase the likelihood your costumed crowd will really "let their hair down," creating the sort of get-togethers that only occur on rare occasion. Accordingly, with a focus on minimizing their intrusion into usable party space, let's take a look at some of the more significant props we've incorporated into our own annual "All Hallows' Eve" gatherings.

# Frankenstein's Castle

## The Grounds

Halloween time prompts the average residence to display appropriate decoration, mostly in the form of scarecrows, skeletons, pumpkins, and the like. While our house may be a little more elaborately adorned, it still blends in quite well with all the others in the neighborhood...at least from the outside. Thus, we feel the need to draw added attention to it for the sake of the party, so we position our official "Greeter" down at the end of the driveway assuring our guests they've indeed arrived at the right address.

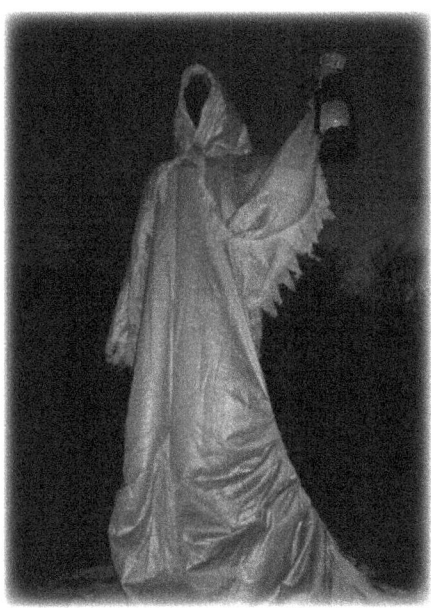

With glowing lantern swinging to and fro, our interactive street-side cloaked friend is sure to stand out, gaining the attention of both our anticipated costumed companions, as well as any passing motorists who happen down the road on this spookiest of nights.

Nothing like whetting our partygoers' appetites for a hauntingly good time by tingling the right nerve endings even before they officially arrive. We begin the night's journey by leading our select visitors through a landscape of surreal sights as they make their way toward the front entrance...such as this poor lost soul, hanging from the cherry tree in our front yard surrounded by numerous assorted oversized cocoons no doubt housing some delicacy to be consumed at a later time by their rightful owner.

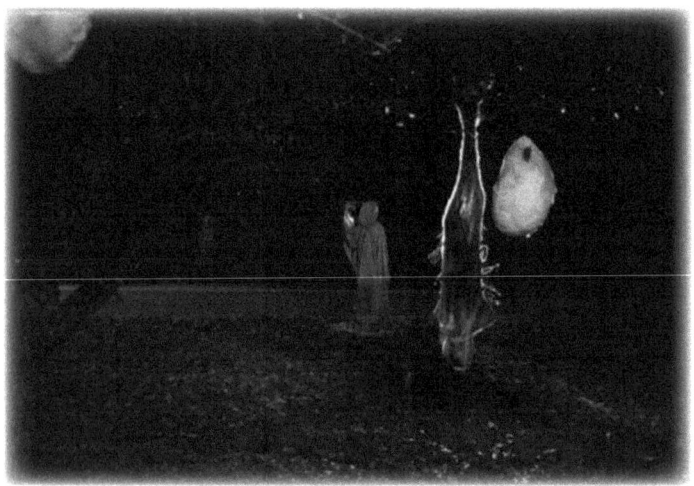

Meanwhile, with lantern in hand to better view his most recent work, our resident Gravedigger ensures that our masquerading masses are getting off on the right foot...strategically placed directly off to one side of the front entrance.

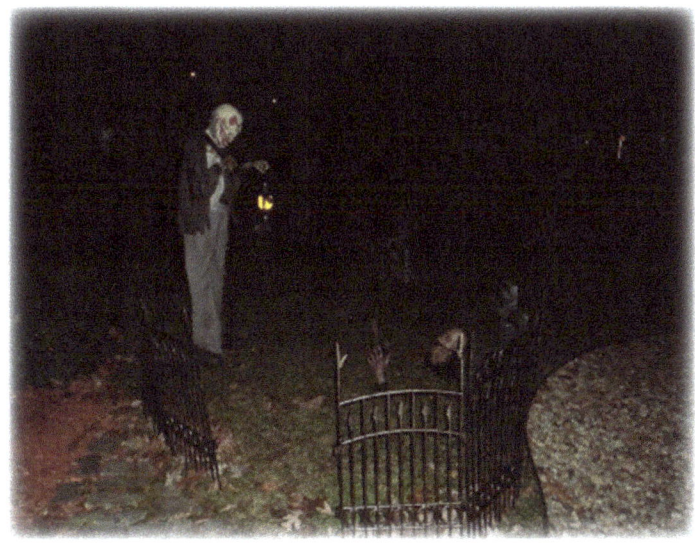

While the items you see here work in concert to create the perfect graveyard scene, they become all the more enhanced when just the right amount of light is cast outward from above the front entranceway. When properly accomplished, appropriate spacing of the headstones gives the illusion of a cemetery with no end.

With our "Greeter" flagging down invited guests at the end of the driveway and a walk up to the front door that runs past a creepy enough graveyard to warrant a second look, the stage has been well-set for things to come on this most special of nights. One thing's for sure, if you've arrived not quite sure if you were in the mood for a Halloween costume party, all doubt is about to be removed!

## Entranceway

Speaking of entrances, upon arrival, our halloweening houseguests become instantly aware they're passing through a veritable portal as they become immediately confronted with a second suspended, cocooned corpse...

this one being clambered over by a number of oversized spiders. Our arachnid's prey is an excellent use of this particular space. Not only does the manner in which it's presented serve to instantly grab the attention of new arrivals, but it's strung up directly over the handrail such that it doesn't interfere with stairwell traffic, not to mention being a focal point of the party remaining clearly visible from up on the first floor where Frankenstein's Castle will rock on into the wee hours.

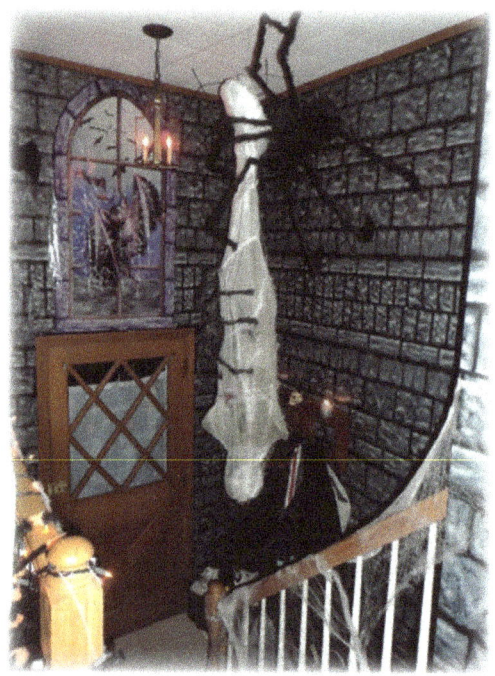

Note the castlelike walls, twelve feet high here in the split-level entryway. In fact, the entire first floor of the house is transformed into a "haunted castle" each Halloween by covering the walls of every room, halls and all, with appropriately patterned reams of wallpaper, completing the perfect atmosphere for the annual gathering of all our favorite ghouls and goblins.

Of course, the decor has been known to change as events have come to pass, in this instance, swapping out our spider's prey with perhaps even a more sinister presence.

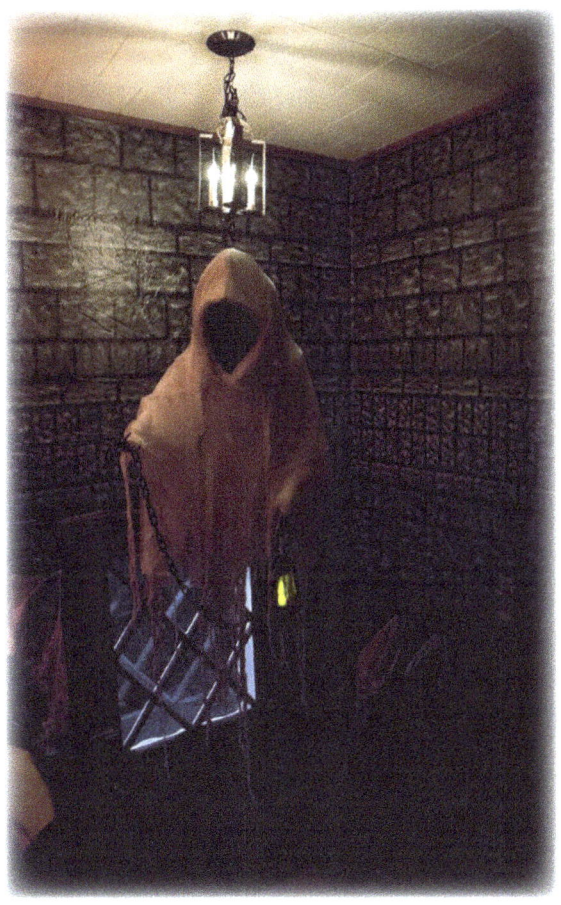

No matter the individual props that are brought into the mix at any given event, as we delve further into our journey you'll discover two distinct ongoing themes—the eye-catching nature of the displays themselves, and the degree of detail and thoughtfulness that goes into the presentation of the final selections.

*NOW* we're talking...addition through subtraction! Under "game conditions" no matter the decoration/prop, the surroundings take on more of a macabre feel. Here we see our hanging friend captured under castlelike "mood" lighting. Once the party begins, all lighting throughout the house is either accomplished via orange-tinted light bulbs, strings of orange LEDs, lit candelabras, or flame pots...adding eerily to the overall haunted castle effect.

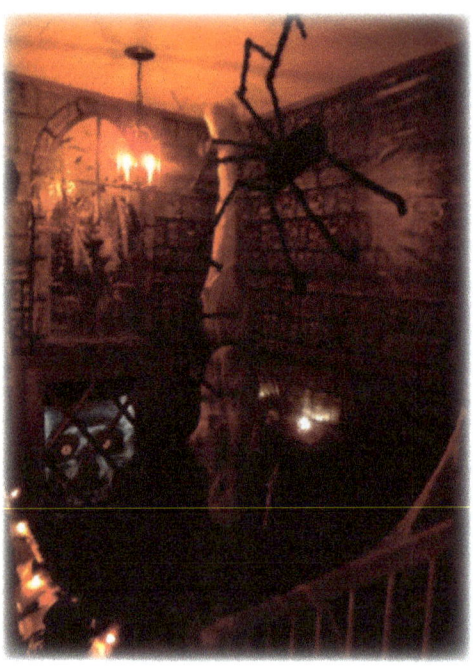

I'm not going to lie...the wallpaper takes a number of hours to hang (longer the first time as you're measuring to length, cutting out holes for light switches, etc.). But once you get past the initial time investment and bag up the custom-made, labeled sections by room, this seemingly massive task goes much quicker than you'd think after the first undertaking. The bottom line is for OUR Halloween playground, this is the single most important step toward creating the perfect environment, a backdrop against which all other additions/props gain depth and eye appeal. For the boorish, it may seem like overkill, but to those looking to escape the nuances of everyday life and be shown a good time, dedicating sufficient prep time makes ALL the difference.

# Common Area

Reaching the top of the staircase, we officially welcome you to Frankenstein's Castle! Not every prop makes the cut when it comes to populating our house of haunts with appropriate ambiance. As you'll see, as you venture further into our castle, while a few fun-type decorations can certainly be found in the mix, most purchases are required to pass muster regarding degree of authenticity, horrific value, and appropriateness for the space available. With little exception, the items that find a place in our "house of Frankenstein," each possess an element of creepiness and originality. Make no mistake about it, this party environment is not meant for little ones but instead attempts to instill a most appropriate horror-movie motif. As such, there remains a purposeful focus on what really "works" versus props that are "happy," plastic looking, or just plain fake.

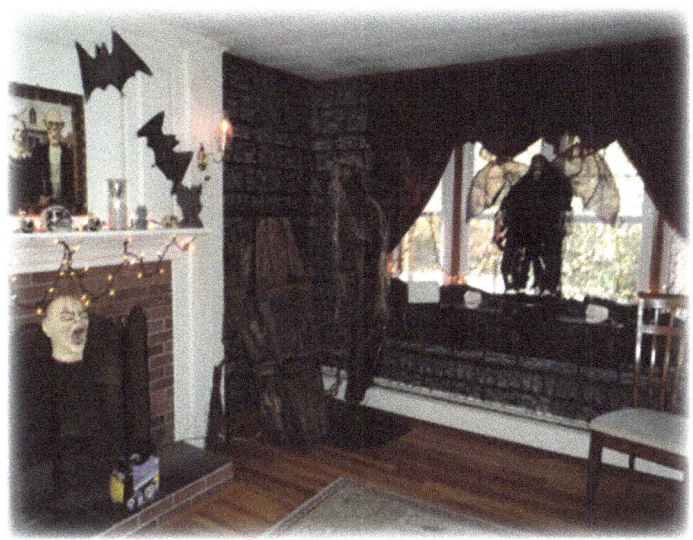

As mentioned, orange mood lighting is sprinkled here and there to "improve" visibility to an acceptable level once the houselights go out come party time. Here, our flying demon makes great use of the recessed bay window area, while gargoyles and remnants of past visitors adorn the fireplace. And who is that "Spectre" in the corner?

Not all props are "plug and play!" When shopping to fill our Halloween playground, we keep the creative juices flowing. Here, we see the marrying up of our uninvited Spectre with a surprisingly realistic 3-D coffin which, while purchased separately, work in concert to enhance the imagery. Get a good look at this guy... even in the daylight, he really is creepy looking.

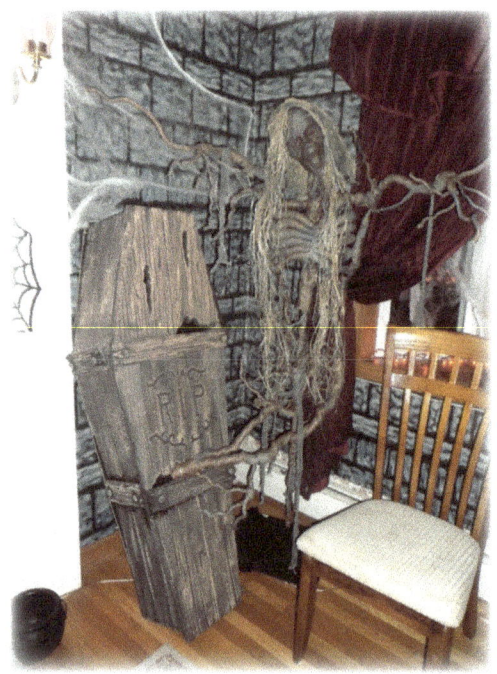

Once the lights dim and mist starts running across the floor via a "fog" machine (on a timer) conveniently hidden beneath the dining room table, it helps to induce a heightened sense of eeriness to this setting. No, we don't miss a trick! Both pieces of this display were discovered at different ends of the same store, making it easier to imagine them complimenting one another in our special effects-ridden-castle environment.

Hosts note: Removal of some of the bulkier furniture allows for extra space to create a greater variety of effects, as well as additional party space. The kids' bedrooms (they won't be home on this "All Hallows' Eve") make for the perfect storage areas for excess items.

Not being one to miss an opportunity to further promote the proper atmosphere, even the fireplace finds itself superbly involved through this simple yet extremely effective display of...postmortem ex-partyers? Regardless, we find the presentation awe-inspiring, making an already uninviting location...even more so.

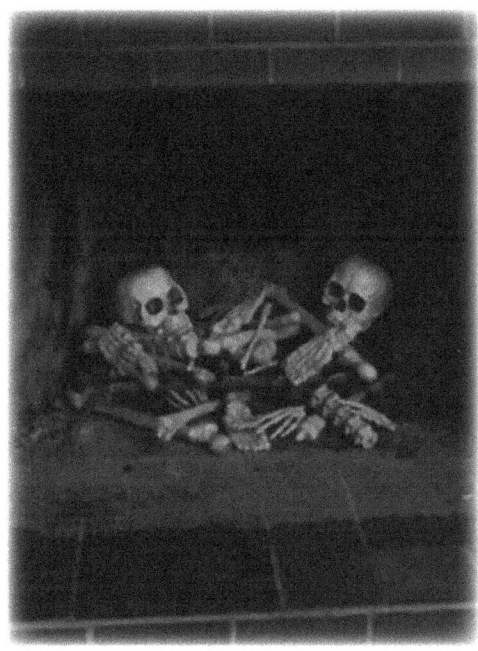

Moving to the left of the fireplace, conveniently located in the "dead space" (pun intended) next to the hutch, we find what no haunted castle would be complete without...a life-sized, fully functioning Mummy!

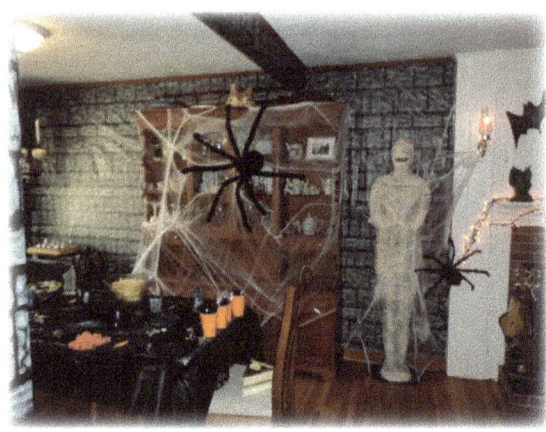

You'll also note that a liberal amount of webbing has been applied throughout our virtual castle, supplemented with the occasional length of undetectable thread taped to the ceiling dropped down to about shoulder height, adding yet another interactive dimension to the overall spidery effect.

Truth be told, there's even a remote-controlled repelling spider (see "Effects/Illusions") that can be found periodically dropping down from its virtually invisible nesting place in the ceiling strategically located in another section of our haunted house once Frankenstein's Castle has been completely transformed. Oh yeah, good times.

As implied, this particular mummy is one of the more interactive participants found within these rather elaborately adorned chambers. Motion activated, once engaged, the eyes light up moving from side to side while a quite audible mumbling continually escapes its mouth, desperately crying out for "help" in an effort to free itself from its meticulously bound condition. A real crowd-pleaser! Note that even the main beam running across the ceiling has been wallpapered. A little over the top, but like I say...that's what this party's all about.

Below we have the finished scene after the lights go out, becoming dramatically more appealing to the average castle dweller's eyes and, better still, their mind-set. Seemingly everywhere you look, there's something new to soak in, adding to the general feeling that this party may yet prove to be somewhat "special." Over the years, we've managed to gather together some extraordinary finds from some of the most unlikely sources. This Mummy is a perfect example, having been purchased from a home improvement center. Well, it certainly improved the house of Frankenstein! Talk about your impulse buys, but I knew when I saw it, we had to have it.

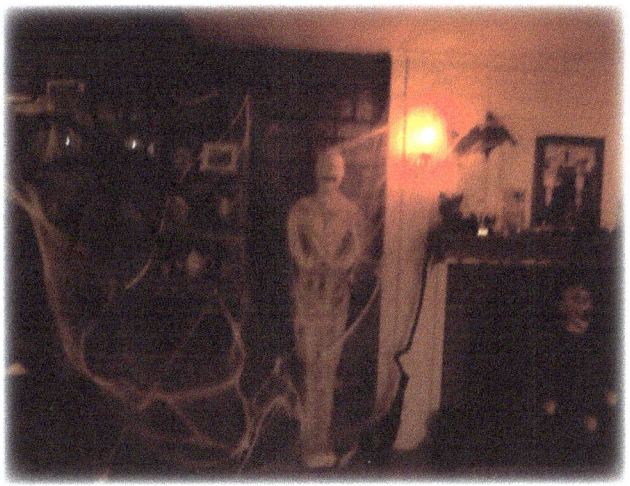

Our resident Mummy is centrally positioned on the far wall of the front-to-back living/dining rooms, allowing for a significant traffic pattern in close enough proximity to maintain his continued involvement throughout the evening's events. After initial inspection, his near nonstop pleas for assistance tend to fade into the background, becoming just another element in the back-drop against which the night's gathering takes place.

It's also fun to note that our daughter doesn't really appreciate this particular prop, insisting that it remain covered with a sheet right up until party time, and it's no wonder...while clearly visibly stimulating, the audible is priceless as well!

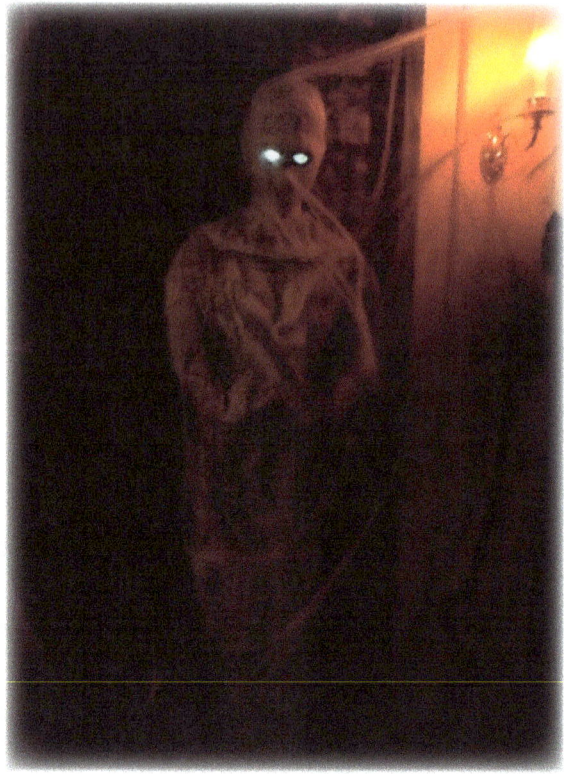

As hinted at thus far, over the course of time, we've made it a point to expand our thought process to include every one of the senses in as many ways as possible. So far, we've combined "mood" lighting, cobwebbed accents, fog, and even "castle-ized" walls, all in an effort to create the perfect "play-ground" in which we perform an annual dance with our favorite demons. To this point, you may simply feel that all this is mildly interesting, but we're just getting started.

# Feast Room

Looking down from the living room into the dining area, the host of the party—Frankenstein himself—can be found seated at the head of our feast table. While bringing added authenticity (and a focal point) to the setting, this prop is nothing more than a mask and a stuffed suit. There continue to be attendees at every party we've ever thrown, who wait for the person inside the mask to move. They wait a long time.

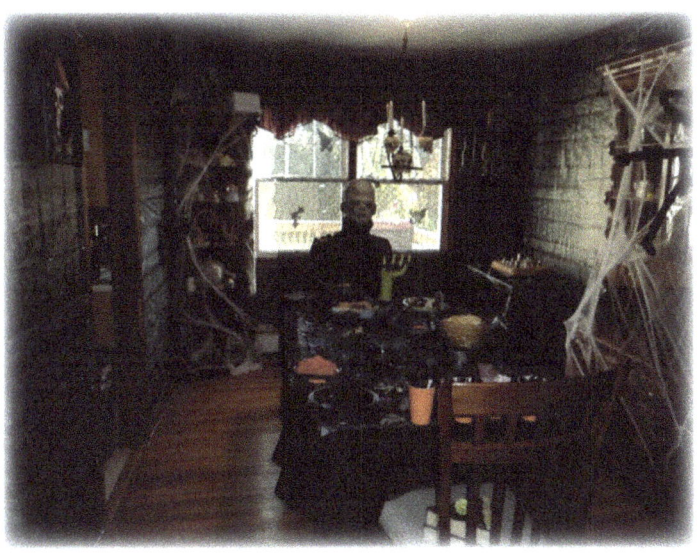

Here, more detail begins to stand out. Check out the real candles burning in the skeleton-head chandelier, the hand holding a spidery invader, the ghoul in the cage hanging from the ceiling, and is that a piece of cake on the chair closest to us? To come clean, I was "Fat Elvis" one year, and that was a homemade prop for my costume. Not everything we have in the castle is store-bought. Over the years, we've done what we can to keep costs down. The biggest secret is to gradually add to its contents each time we throw the party. What you're seeing in these pages is the accumulation of items gathered over several Halloween events. By adding each year, we attempt to make the party new for the die-hards that always attend, not to mention heightening the overall experience for any "newbies" that get thrown into the mix.

Under party-time lighting, Frankenstein looks more ominous than ever, making the dining room a great gathering place to load up with some tasty treats. Remember, he's nothing more than a costume stuffed with rags (the bulkier, the better) with his outer clothing safety pinned together. A wooden post runs through his core from his seat to his head and he's belted into position in his chair to guarantee sufficient rigidity. Sitting at the head of our food table, in this setting, he certainly looks real enough to warrant a double take.

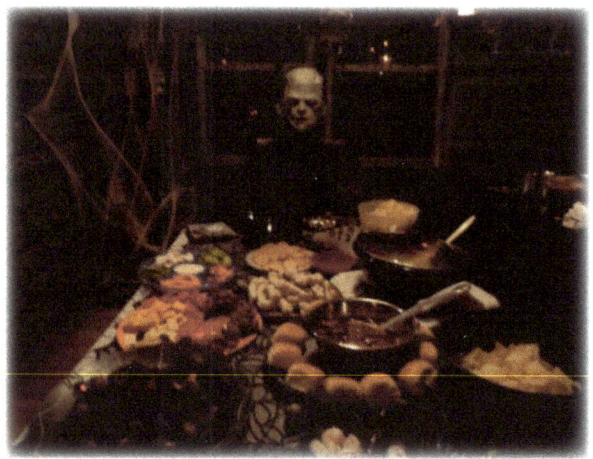

Of course, we would never leave out the menu (see "Food" section) when it comes to adding an extra helping of theme to the event. Some of our favorites include different variations of what we lovingly refer to as "finger food," bones and blood (appropriately shaped biscuits/marinara sauce), eyeball punch, graveyard cake, mummy dogs, and my personal favorite, the "litter box" (rectangular cakelike creation covered in sand-mimicking topping with "squirts" of Tootsie Roll sprinkled about with a serving spatula that's an actual kitty litter scoop). Mmmm, yum!

# The Dungeon

Wandering still further into our house of horrors, as promised, we're running a fully operational castle here with all the trimmings! Welcome to the room that without which no castle is complete, the "dungeon!" While we're certain most of our cloaked companions experience an exceptionally good time when playing in Frankenstein's Castle, we can't speak for those from past events who weren't allowed to leave.

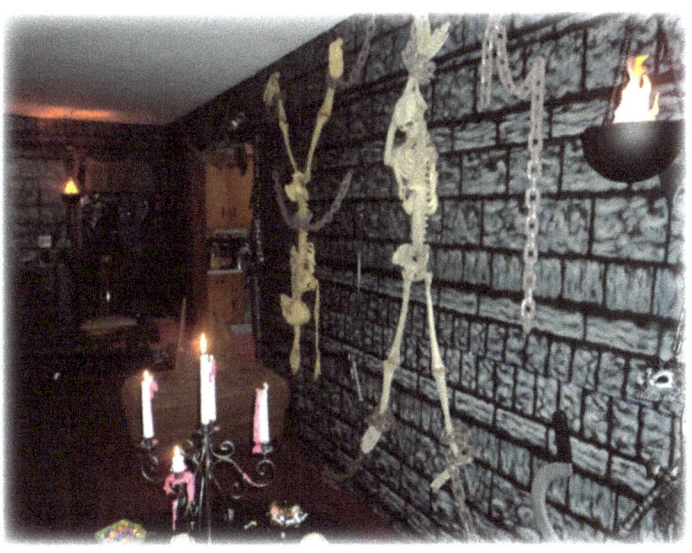

Somewhat exorbitantly demonstrating an excellent use of wall space, our virtual "dungeon" is appropriately outfitted with a "torture chamber" including victims, weaponry, hanging flame pots, assorted lengths of chain, etc., all of which can be located at most Halloween stores of significance. But when you bring it all together and present it in the proper context, it produces a clear-cut theme to this particular party room, one that plays to the castle's inner workings. And yes, this room always proves to be another main attraction while also providing the perfect setting for some of our game time events (see "Games" section).

Same scene with the lights out. Now you're getting the idea! It's all an illusion, but a grand one indeed! Remember, there are two stereo systems playing simultaneously throughout the castle. Our dungeon features a surround sound system that booms out a thunderstorm throughout the night, adding yet one more level of demonic delight to torture chamber visitors. As mentioned (foot pedal activated) floodlights mounted outside directed at the windows add to this effect. Flame pots are of particular intrinsic value here, casting just the right amount of glow from the corners of the chamber. Mix in the thunderstorm and what you have here is one runaway party!

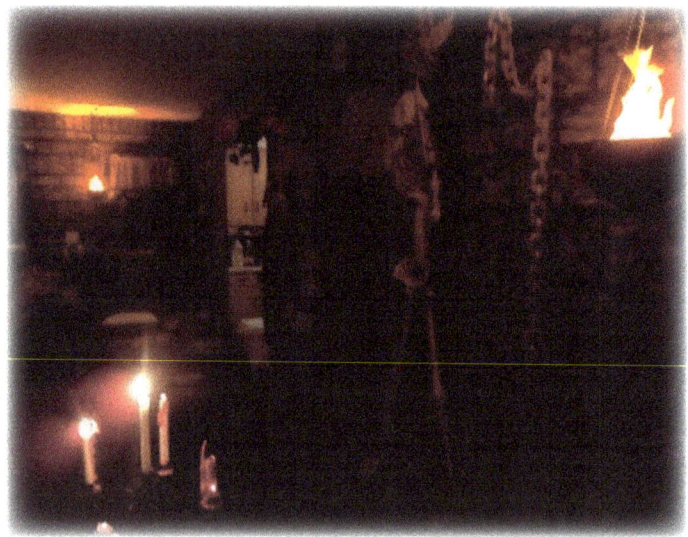

Here, a picture is truly worth a thousand words. As a guest, at some point in your journey through this night, it eventually dawns on you...that YOU, in whatever costume you've chosen for yourself, serve as just another prop in this most surreal of settings. You find yourself drifting much farther away than the two-block walk from your house. It's then that you begin to lose yourself in this freak show of a party as the full transformation now begins to get underway. It's all we wanted all along...for our guests to release. On this night to become a little separated from the norm, to rid themselves of worldly tension and ultimately...BRING THE PARTY!

Adding to our list of major props, the opposite wall of the torture chamber boasts a mourning widow who is seen here, facing all of eternity clutching a bouquet of black roses. Note the black lace draped over the existing curtains to assist in blending them with the decor. The castle's walls are further adorned with a selection of artwork, portraits of family members/previous castle owners who (of course) change into ghouls and goblins as one alters their vantage point. Articulate positioning of weaponry over this particular piece of artwork adds to the overall feel of the dungeon. As mentioned, while some furniture gets removed for the sake of creating additional space, other pieces simply get rearranged... in this instance, not only to allow full access to the poor hanging souls on the torture chamber's main wall opposite our widow...

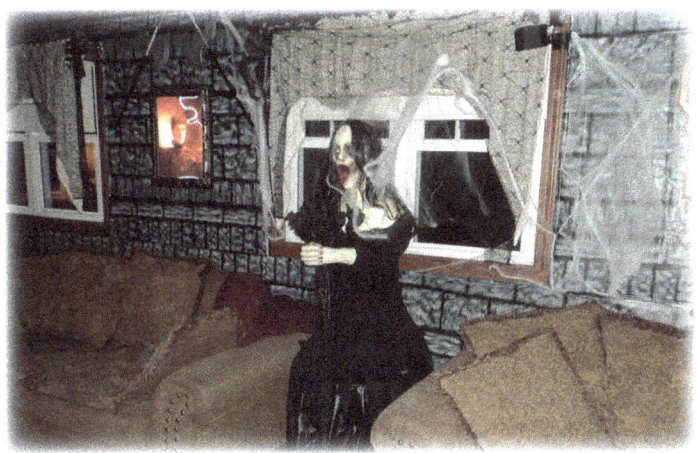

......but with the center of the dungeon area opened up, this party space also doubles as our castle's game room. It should be noted here that when it comes time to subjecting our masquerading mob to any one of our creative play time events (see "Games"), while the surround sound system continues to roar out a thunderous storm, the house stereo switches from an eighties hard rock theme to Frankenstein's favorite castle offering, "Toccata in D minor." Look it up! It's classic haunted house organ music that when played against the backdrop of our thunderstorm, well, you get the picture...details...details! More on games coming up!

Below is another example of matching up props to produce a combined effect, as well as illustrating more creative use of available space. In earlier parties, we didn't incorporate the TV at all (which is located at the far end of our "dungeon"), but it always seemed that it should be involved somehow. Then we came across a CD package that included a black veil that went over the TV screen behind which the heads of monsters/assorted lost souls seemingly float in midair while rambling on about this or that. And that was fine for one party.

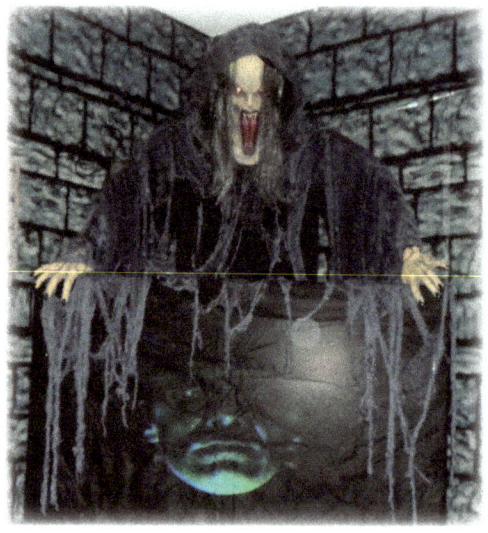

But then we found this pretty horrific looking witch. So to complete the effect, we've positioned the witch behind/above the TV, looking down with arms and hands extended as if to be summoning up the head that floats beneath it. And the whole setup doesn't take up any party room! Now that's my idea of another great use of available space—not to mention the eerily ghoulish influence it brings to the chamber in which it resides.

# The Hall

After partaking in enough refreshment, one eventually finds the urge to locate the castle's restroom. But something or "someone" lurks in the (not too) distant darkness! What madness is this? Arguably the best prop in Frankenstein's Castle, this frightful piece of rubber is the ultimate attention grabber under "game conditions" residing in our house of haunts down at the end of the centrally located hallway.

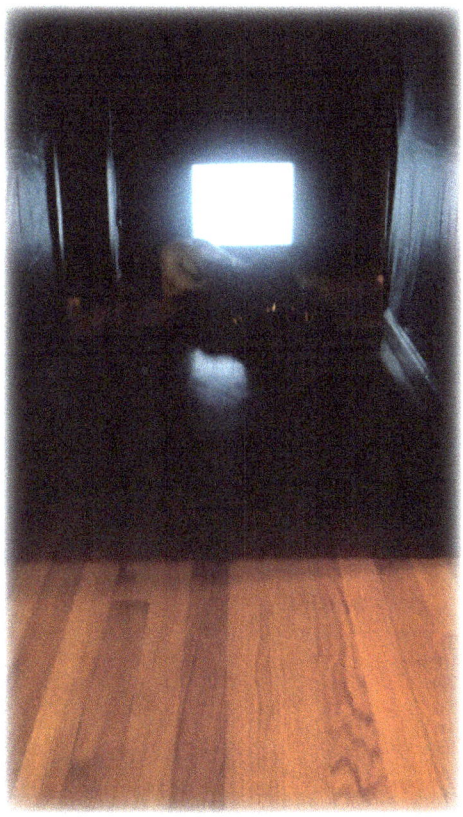

Ratcheting up the overall horrific feel of our haunted castle yet another notch, this creepy crawler is carefully positioned with lit bedroom doors purposefully left slightly ajar on her left (by her butt), as well as on her right (by her face). With no other light available but from the static on the TV behind this gruesome little goulette, and the bedroom doors cracked open just so...offering but a glimpse of her butt, face, and hands...she looks quite intimidating, stopping every one of our partygoers in their tracks before they ever reach their destination—the bathroom, halfway down the hall.

We even recall an actual screech or two from some of our weaker guests, adding yet another dimension of sound effect throughout the castle's chambers. This prop always proves to be quite the attraction and well worth the investment as at least initially each of our partying peers gingerly approaches one by one to ensure its artificial nature. But better still, the closer you get, the more real she seems to become! This particular addition to our haunted castle serves as yet another reminder that you need to keep an eye out for what really works when it comes to populating your available party space. Although I never pictured being able to incorporate a "hall of horror" with such great success, as soon as this prop caught my eye, I envisioned immediately how I could display it to ramp up our dungeon party another degree or two. For parties past, the hallway was simply a passage to the bathroom. This little creature not only makes the hall part of the event but remains our single biggest attention grabber. I have to admit, this one wasn't exactly cheap, but was it worth it? Collectively, our garbed guests all scream YES!

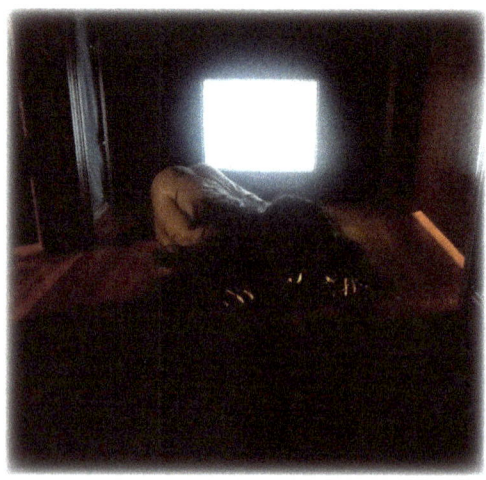

This was truly a one of a kind find as there was only one available in the store, and the owner did not know of another to be had. So lesson learned . . . remain alert! Keep your creative mind in tune and your eyes wide open! This particular purchase changed the "dead space" at the end of the hall into one of our most desired attractions!

## The Bathroom

Speaking of idle space, it turns out that NO room is safe on this "All Hallows' Eve." The main course for Frankenstein's feast (come to find out our frolicking friends have all been invited to a wild boar roast) provides for a double whammy of excitement after just getting over the creepy chick crawling down the hallway. Have a seat and relax, the boar's head only twitches once in a while!

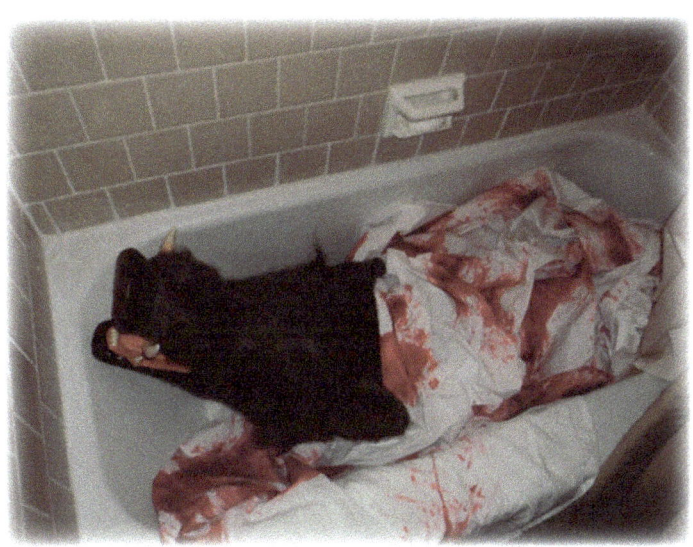

Again, you never know when you're going to come across the perfect prop for your available space! This boar's head may have been a little steep for our budget also, but how were we supposed to pass on this one? Wrapped in a homemade bloody sheet, the main course for tonight's feast looks right at home. This is yet another example of "the closer you get, the more real it looks!" When's the last time crowds of people gathered in YOUR bathroom? Frankenstein doesn't have that problem as ghouls and goblins alike flock to see for themselves this most grand of props adding to the growing list of extravagant items on display throughout Frankenstein's haunted castle (and once again, using up zero party space). At least where this effect is concerned, the best is usually saved for last. After the initial excitement of the tub's contents wears off, some attendees show up later after most have moved on from any associated shock factor. Inevitably, at some distant point in the night, a shriek will be heard from the restroom area as some unfortunate soul gets introduced to our boar's head for the first time—unannounced! And we simply adore the addition of realistic screams to the halls of the "house of Frankenstein" mid-party!

Now that you've gotten a feel for the types of things we look for when selecting the more significant props (as well as their presentation), before we move on, let's take a closer look at some of the details we left out along the way starting with what we might term "filler" items we may have missed through our initial tour.

# Detail

## Additional Props

This is "Agatha." I should mention that when Agatha made her initial appearance, we lived in what we understood to be the third oldest house in town. The aged place boasted an oversized, centrally located chimney with fireplaces upstairs in the master bedroom, on the ground floor in the living room and kitchen, as well as down in the basement that all had a number of odd cutouts with assorted iron eyebolts/hooks for fastening cooking kettles to back in the day. When Agatha showed up in our house for the first time, I told the neighbor's kid that we found her in a hole in the oversized kitchen fireplace wall. His wide-eyed response was a priceless "Really?"

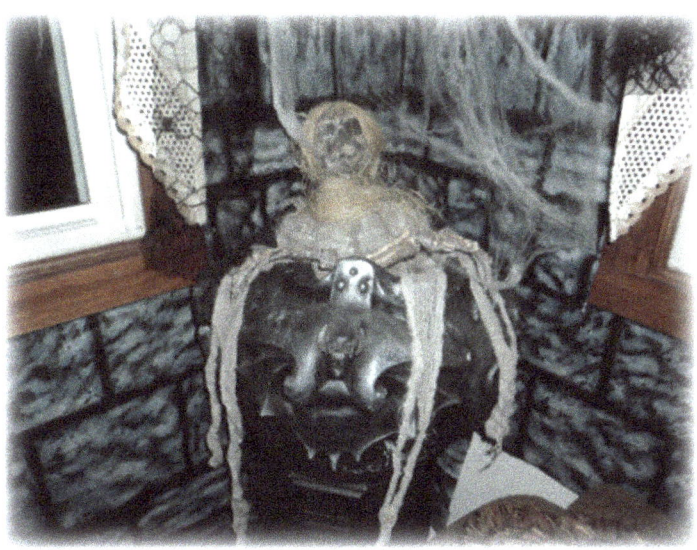

While the story of Agatha's origination may or may not be historically correct, it remains the stuff of dungeon lore. One thing's for sure, she's certainly found a home here in our haunted castle where she continues to be on annual display, occupying one of our more elaborate cauldrons.

Here, a caged ghoul helps to add depth to the castle's feast room, looking right at home, suspended from the ceiling off to the right behind where Frankenstein sits, lit up ominously from behind by one of numerous flame pots that have been meticulously placed throughout the castle's chambers.

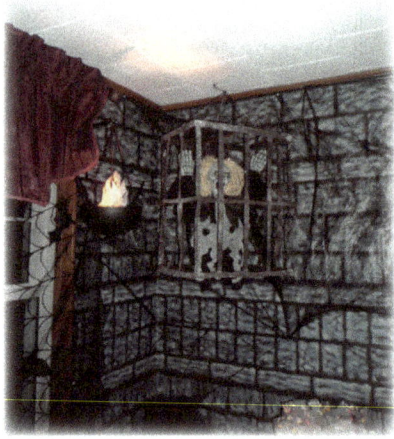

While this tentacle head mounted above a doorway is simply a reminder to our masked minions that they're a long way from home.

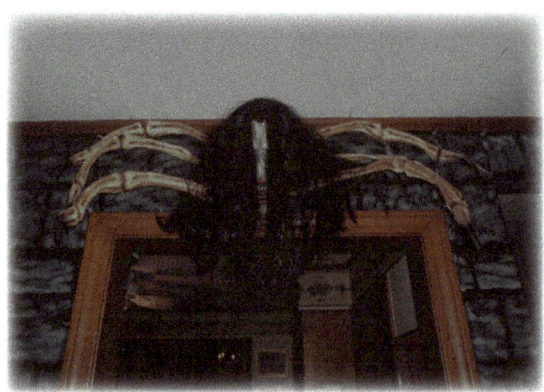

On this particular night, our doorman (Grim Reaper) stepped inside from out in the graveyard for a moment to check out the festivities. He should have no trouble "blending."

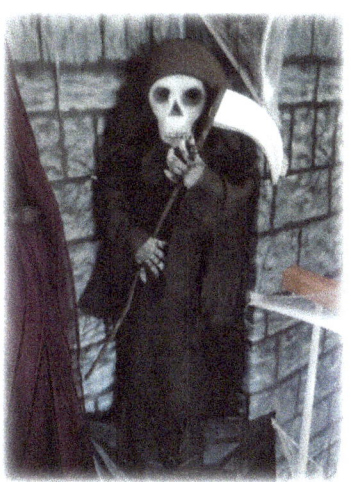

Sound activated, we found "Pumpkin Head" horrific enough to warrant an invite to our annual gathering as well. Once engaged, he rocks to and fro, arms swaying back and forth, with eyes lighting up while he bellows out the most sinister of laughs.

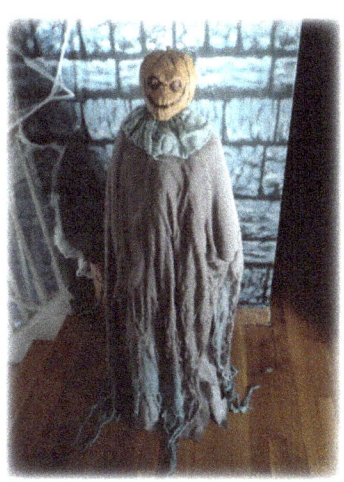

This chained head also passed the authenticity test, finding a home above Frankenstein's fireplace, an apparent warning of the contents that reside therein.

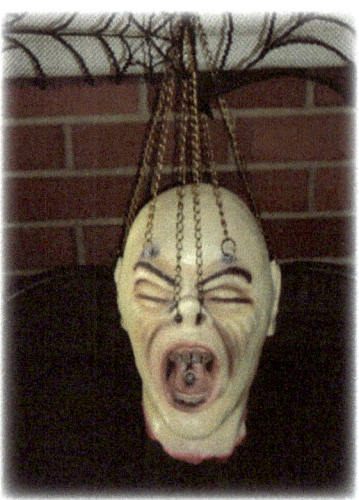

Speaking of heads, we've found that there's something about one in a jar that unnerves a lot of folks. While the components of this particular prop are store-bought, this specialty item was created at home and can be comprised of almost any subject matter, the options being endless.

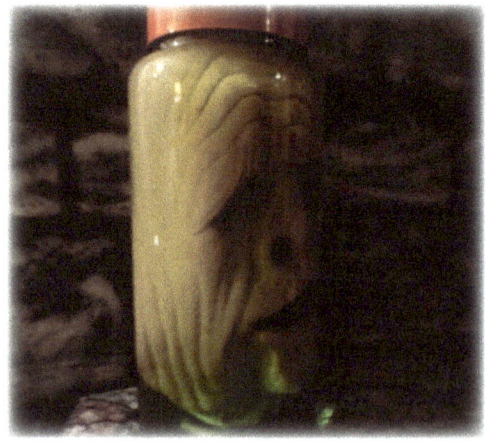

Here's another one...with more examples found later in our "food section," the origins of which coming right out of Frankenstein's laboratory.

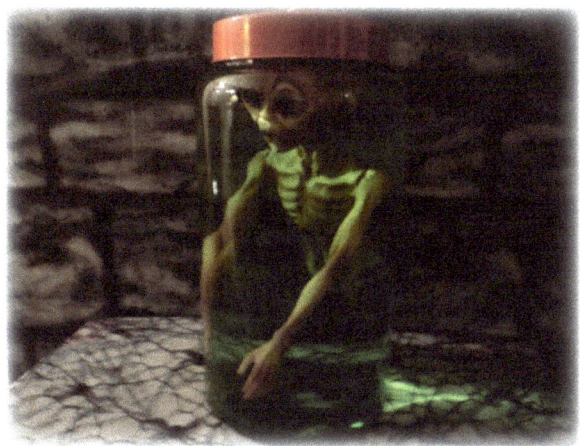

In keeping with the theme of strange things found in jars, among the assorted minutia you'll find throughout our castle playground are these appropriately labeled serums placed here and there on tables, mantles, the beverage bar, etc. The set was quite inexpensive, making the investment in additional detail well worth it.

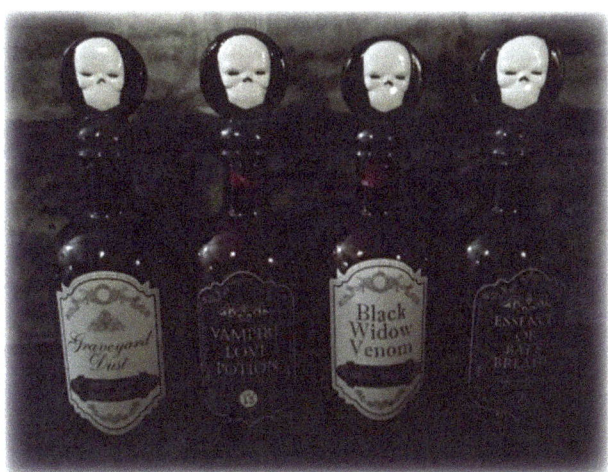

Our 3-D pirate picture is one more interactive piece to help keep our captive audience, well...captivated. Although you have to manually push a button to initiate the talking "pirate skeleton," he IS entertaining...blurting out inquiries about this or that, only to respond to his own questions while his eyes bulge out for effect.

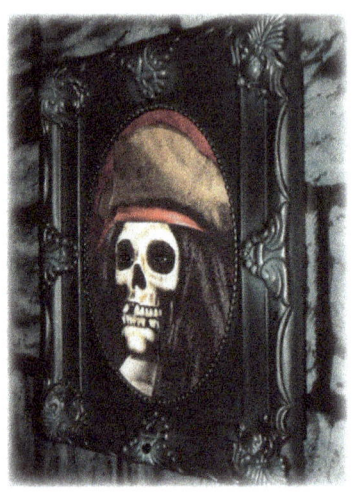

Some props/effects require elaboration, whether to explain the intricacies of how it functions or perhaps why it's worthy enough of placement at our party. Not this one. This is simply a castle-sized rodent. Nuff said. But note the more genuine look over similar rodent likenesses, keeping the "expectation bar" set at an acceptable level.

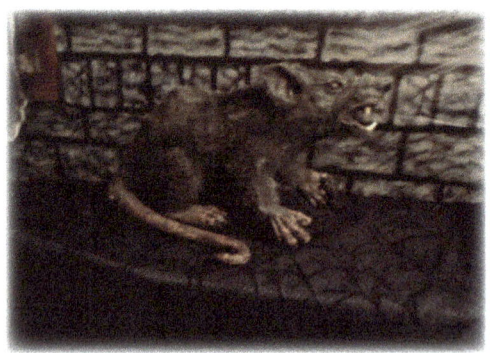

Snakes and skulls, they go together like peanut butter and jelly, don't they? So why bring it up here when there's nothing particularly creative about them? It's because of the snakes. They're pretty straightforward enough...made of wood, cheap enough to buy, etc. The thing about them is the "action." When you handle them, the movement they produce is very realistic. My wife has never appreciated the species, and she definitely does not appreciate these little guys either. Just thought I'd mention it. That and because of their realistic serpentlike motion, they make for additional interactive toys that are fun for our party guests to mess with.

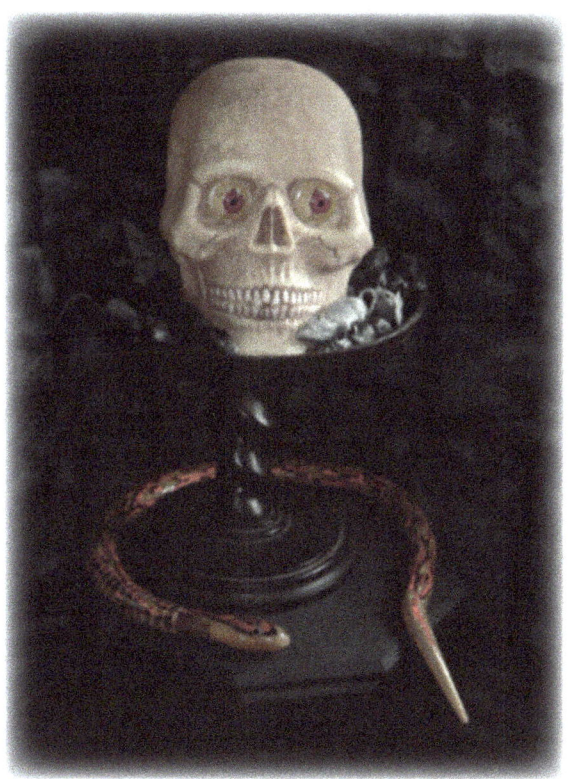

And while we're on skulls, this next glowing one possesses gruesome enough qualities to make the cut as well. Worth noting here, however, is the fact that while we allow this particular props' internal light to remain on, we're not as impressed with every item that lights up or makes a "scary" noise, disconnecting many such attributes and focusing instead on any given props more authentic characteristics.

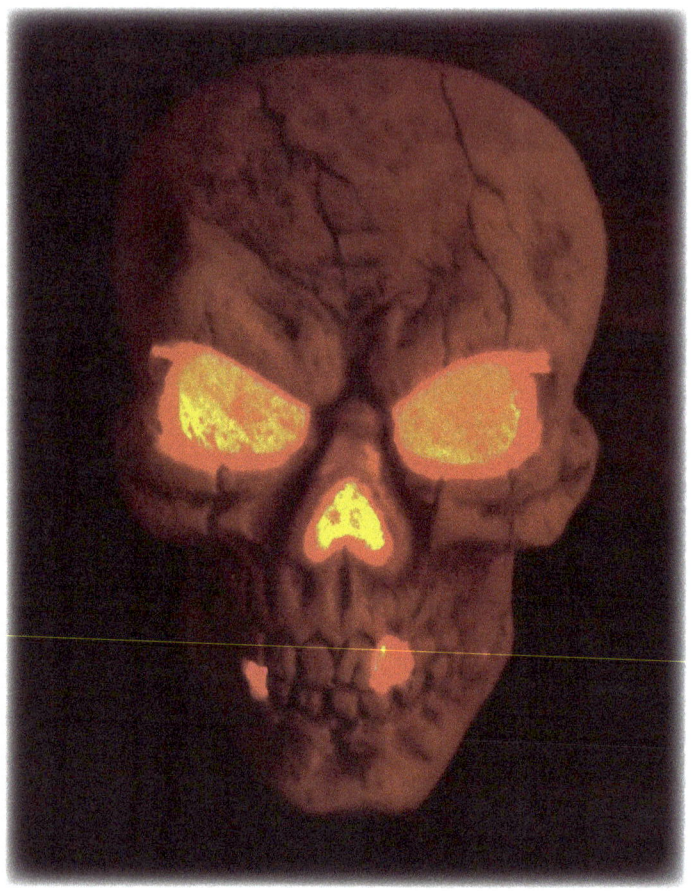

Meanwhile, whenever opportunity knocks to further supplement our haunted castle with interactive playthings, we jump at the chance, this time with a motorized wolf spider that appears real enough in the next pic to warrant the attention he deserves, especially when mobile. Another partygoer favorite.

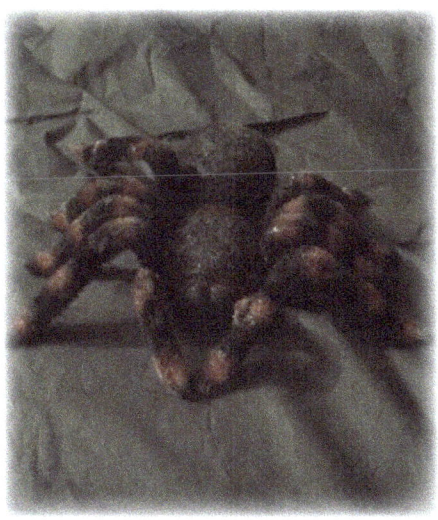

Not being out of place at all in our haunted castle (as its origins can easily be traced to that of witch and warlock lore) is Harry Potter's "Sorting Hat." Initially used for pulling names out of to pick teams at game time before we defaulted to guys versus girls, this prop is now simply the holder of all votes for the best costume award given out toward the end of the night... while also serving as one more item our dungeon dwellers are free to play with throughout each event.

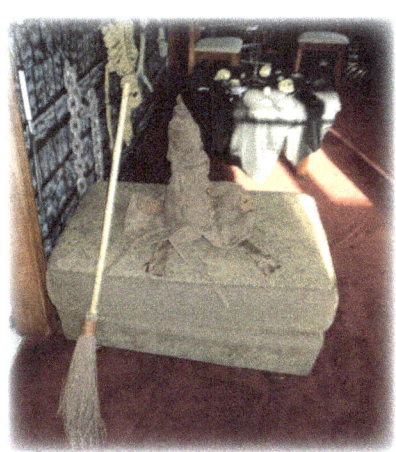

A set of castle-sized keys can be found hanging on the wall just outside of our dungeon. After all, what kind of a torture chamber would we be running if its occupants were allowed to come and go as they please?

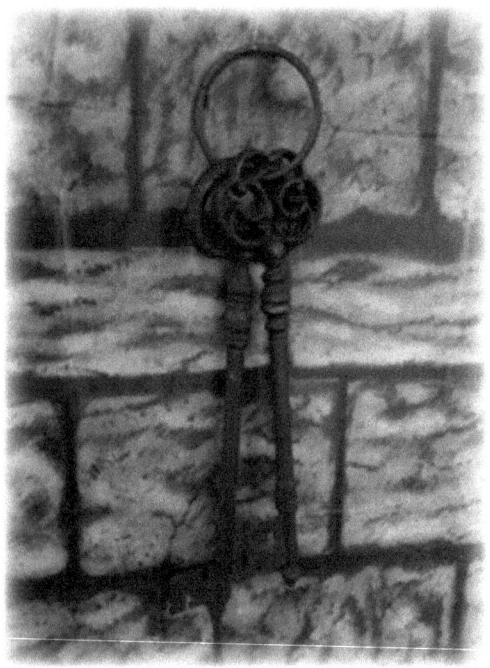

Gargoyles, you gotta love 'em. The good news is that I don't think they make a bad one, and they're cheap! Whether they're made of Styrofoam or stone, they all look good and add appropriate, realistic detail to our haunted castle environment. We have a couple of smaller ones adorning either end of the mantle over the fireplace....

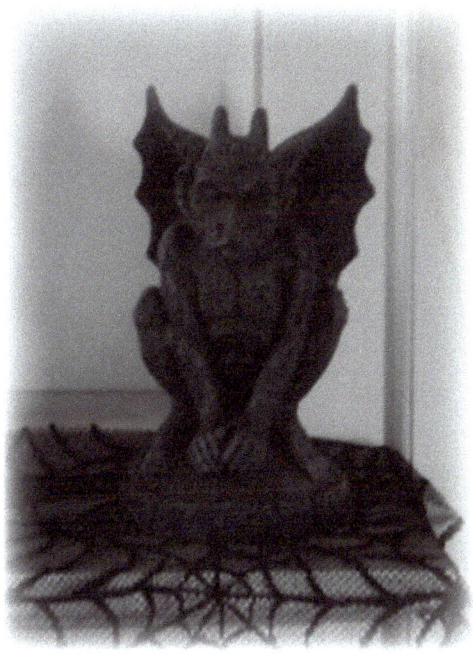

...and this large one, sitting on top of a spider-webbed curio cabinet in the left corner of the dining room behind where Frankenstein sits at the head of the feast table.

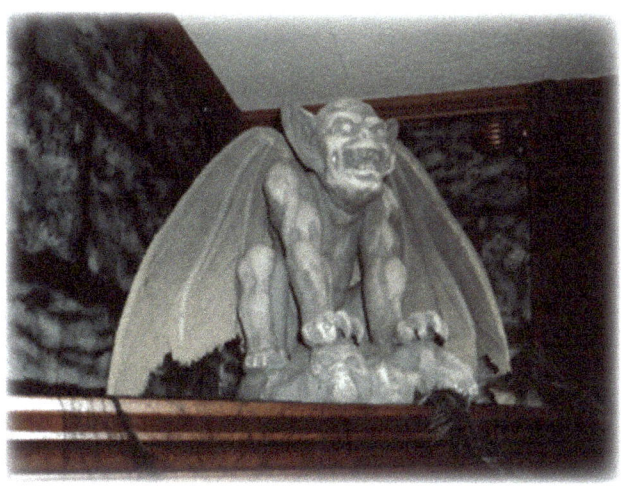

This alien skull is a more recent find, discovered in some "odds and ends" specialty shop. He too is obviously most welcome.

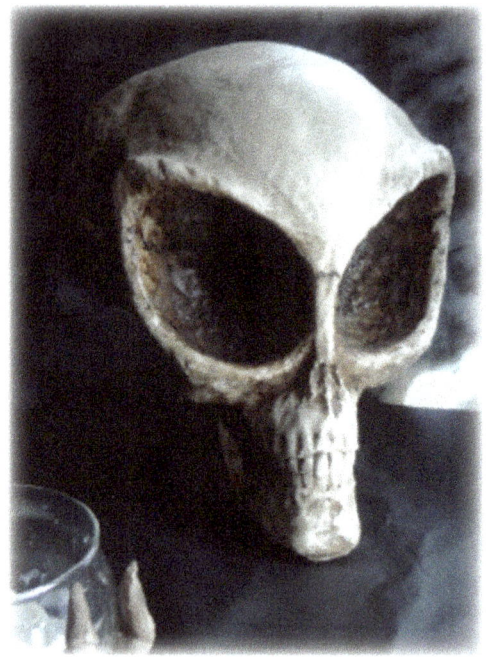

As is this skeleton's bust and assorted adornments...

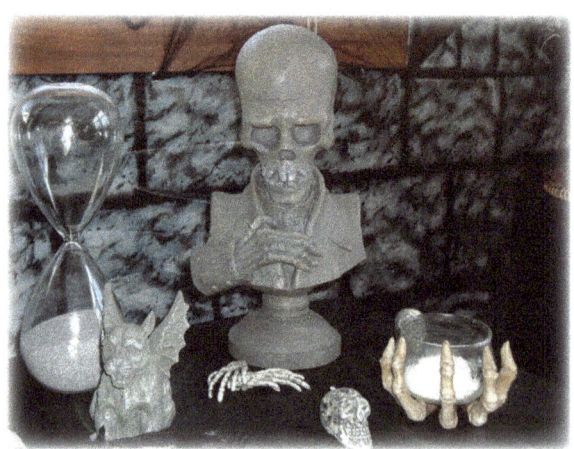

...coming together all too nicely for a quite natural-looking haunt-ed-castle table spread.

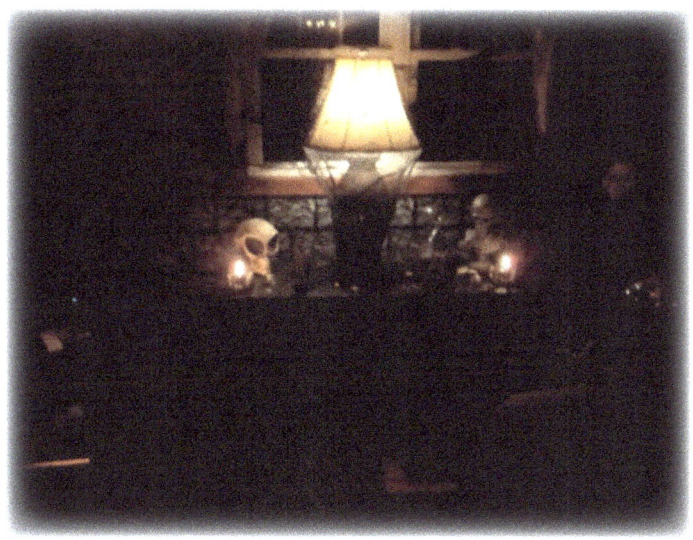

More creaturelike detail added to the mix...

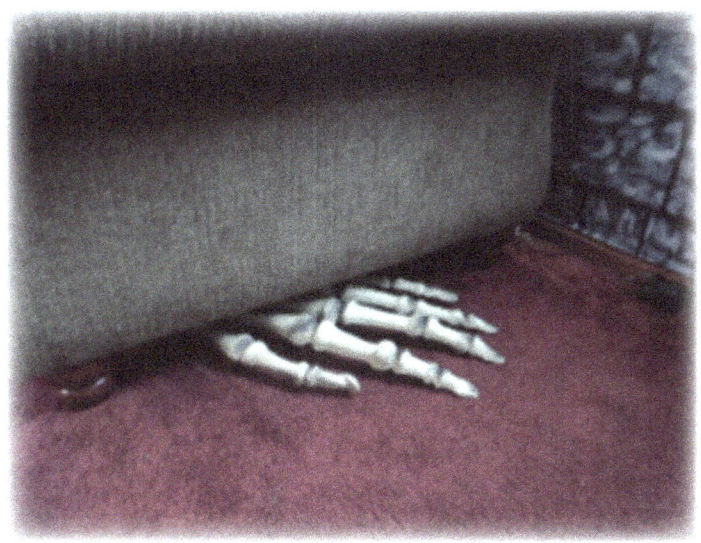

And let's not forget the existing cabinetry, refilled to Frankenstein's exact specifications...a good example of taking what you've got and working with it.

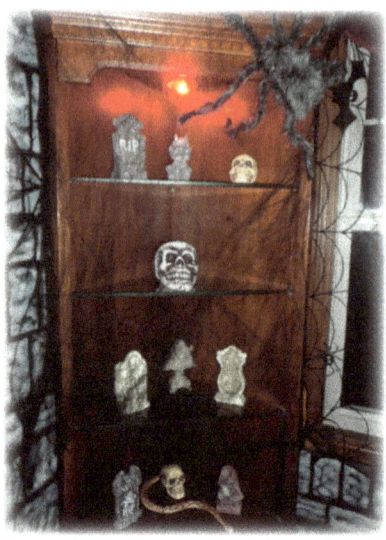

Finally, it's worth mentioning that while our list of supporting props on display here is not necessarily all-inclusive, it's reflective of the types of items that can be found strewn about our Halloween playground, adding castle-appropriate detail while helping to round out our collection of fiendish findings. Whatever devilish assortment of dungeon decor you conjure up, we highly recommend a similar mind-set throughout the procurement process.

Complementing our somewhat extensive list of props are a just as impressive collection of special effects and illusions. To further entertain our partying peers, Frankenstein's Castle also boasts the following additional refinements.

# Effects

First, we can't overlook the obvious, the castle's primary effect which literally encompasses each of our guests in every chamber—the wallpaper. The stonewalled backdrop does a superb job of creating the very environment "against which all other additions/props gain depth and eye appeal." Subsequently, the wall covering in and of itself stands as our number 1 effect. From there, we add the others starting with the lighting.

## Internal Lighting

Aside from orange-tinted strings of LEDs wrapped around railings and draped around window openings and the such, there are a number of alternative light sources casting just the right amount of eerie visibility chamber to chamber. We have:

Focused lighting—purposefully directed on our favorite "ghoulette" at the end of the hall.

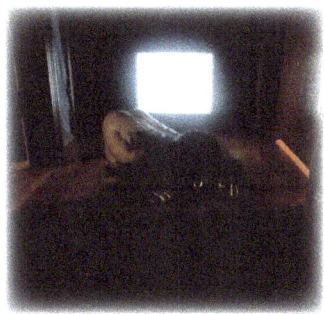

Flame pots scattered here and there, dancing additional life into each castle gathering.

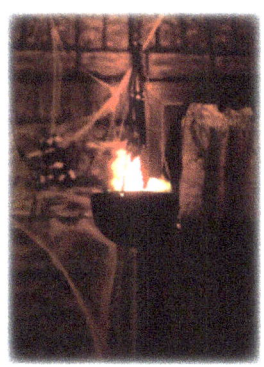

Sconces/assorted candles.

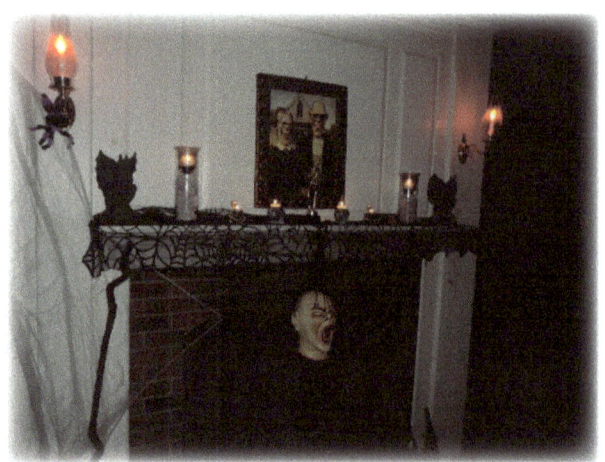

Candelabras

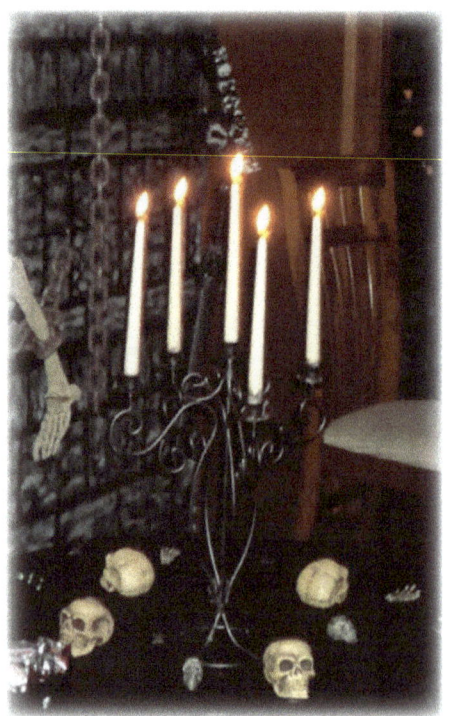

And chandeliers

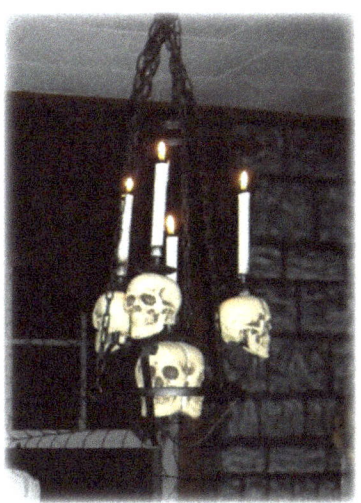

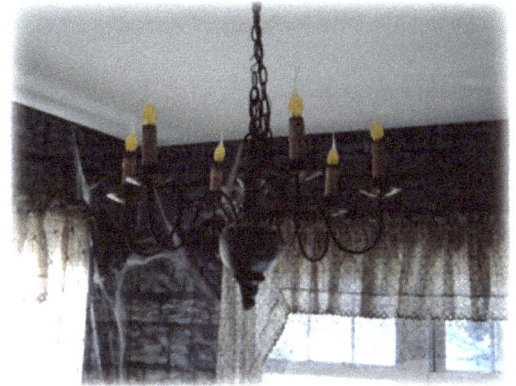

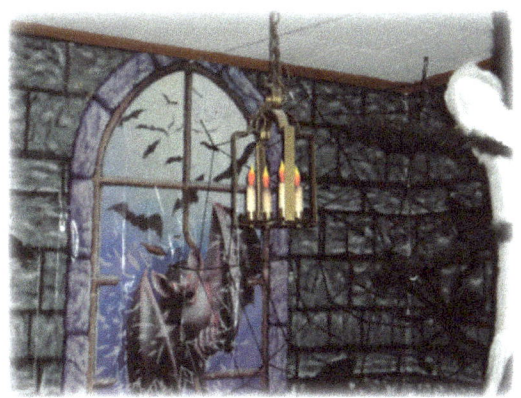

All of the above mentioned items work in concert to help dull one's sense of vision to such an extent that separation of what's real from what's not begins to become a challenge. In the end, the limited lighting plays a major role in allowing our throng of thrill seekers to more easily let their guard down and start to mentally separate themselves from the "norm" in their wickedly wondrous party surroundings.

## External Lighting

Lanterns—We can't exclude the handheld lighting our Greeter (swaying back and forth) and Gravedigger each possess out on the front lawn as they definitely add a subtle element of spookiness to their presence.

The Graveyard—As hinted at earlier, the light bulb in the fixture above the front entrance gets swapped out for one that allows just enough wattage to illuminate the graveyard scene off to the left of the doorway while not readily allowing visitors to determine where the headstones come to an end.

Virtual Lightning—Light show anybody? Our virtual lightning setup may be primitive but extremely effective nonetheless. Using ordinary items found around the house (scrap lumber, extension cords, and floodlights), we've constructed the means through which our castle's party thunderstorm is more than adequately complemented...with flashes of externally produced "lightning." Triggered by a foot pedal (concealed under an overstuffed piece of furniture) lightning bolt flashes light up our dungeon/torture chamber located in the rear of the castle. If you've never had the pleasure of listening to a thunderstorm through the speakers of a surround sound system, let's just say that when coupled with flashes of "lightning" from outside, the overall effect (particularly when standing in our dimly lit torture chamber) is, in a word, spectacular!

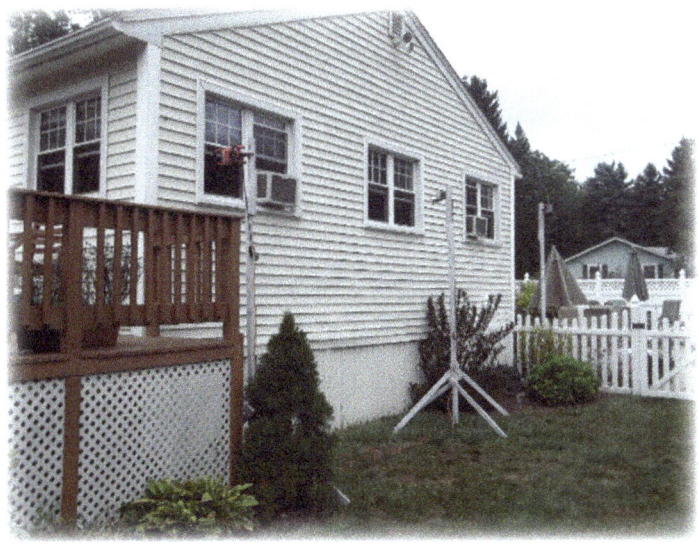

## Audio

Eighties Rock Music—Our eighties rock theme was of course selected as a direct result of knowing our audience and customizing the playlist accordingly. It's suggested that you do the same. While an attempt was made to arrange the chosen songs to help promote the ramping up of the party as it progresses, significant effort was also spent on adding appropriate Halloween-themed sound effects throughout its duration (the result of which is more thoroughly discussed in our "Music" section).

Organ Music—Since we're mentioning audio effects, although it may just be considered part of the music, an effect is an effect! When it's time for our frolicking friends to come out and take part in any one of our Halloween-themed contests, the music (still against the backdrop of the thunderstorm) switches to "Toccata in D minor." This is classic haunted house organ music at its best, providing just the assist we need to properly set the stage and get our houseguest's competitive mind-sets engaged. To say that this little change-up in audio offerings simply produces an effect is at best an understatement.

Thunder—What kind of a lightning storm would it be without thunder? The thunderstorm that ensues on our surround sound system throughout the party we consider to be a necessity. After all, a dungeon party without a thunderstorm would be like a vampire without fangs.

Additional Sound—We have to at least mention the numerous items/props that also emit eerie audible such as the static on the TV behind our hallway "ghoulette," "pumpkin head's" sinister laugh, our muffled Mummy, pirate skeleton, the floating heads on the TV screen, etc. Which is not to say we should leave out our attention-grabbing air horn/cowbell come game time!

Visual

Fog—Eerie mist definitely adds to the overall "aura" of our castle environment; thus, our fog machine also rates high on our list of special effects. We conceal it beneath Frankenstein's feast table and direct timed, released "fog" from the dining area out toward the open living space. Hosts note: The timer is essential as we've discovered that only partially obscuring the immediate vicinity can be a somewhat temperamental thing to achieve.

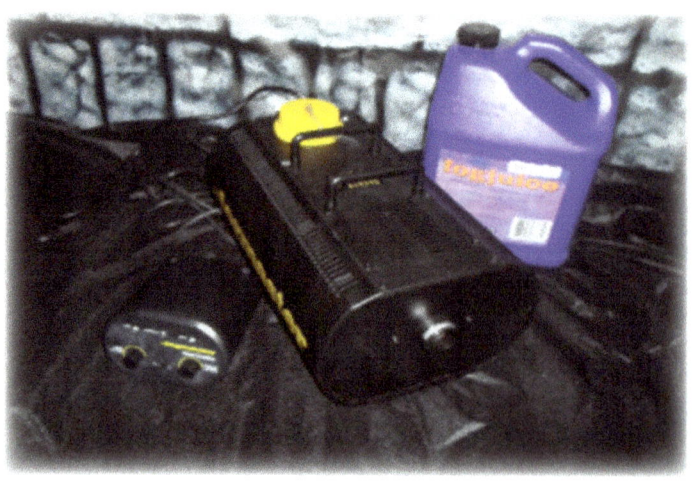

Cobwebs

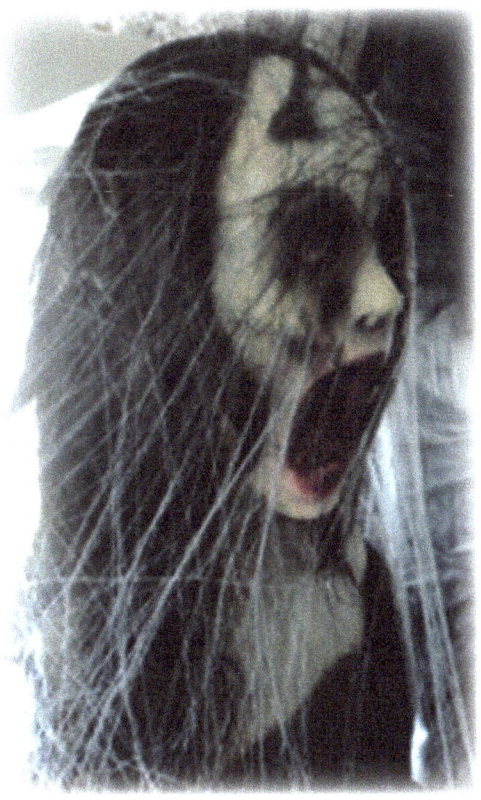

It's well-known that when you come to one of our Halloween bashes, you see a lot of spider webbing inside the halls of our castle, whether it be draped across walls, furniture, bookcases, lampshades, Mummies, whatever. Not as well-known is the fact that hidden fans are pointed across the walls aimed to waft any (purposefully left loose) webbing, further promoting the overall spidery, spooky feel of a drafty castle. Truth be told, the fans actually serve multiple additional purposes including keeping the crowd a degree cooler, as well as circulating the "vampire's blood" aroma throughout our castle's party rooms. "Vampire's blood," you say? What might we be talking about here...?

## Extra Sensory

Aromatic Ambiance—Okay, we might be going a little off the deep end now, but an out of the way visit to an official "witch's store" had us not being able to leave without a few significant purchases. We have yet to discuss the very air that our outfitted outcasts are subjected to while visiting Frankenstein's Castle, but just as sure as we're out to exhilarate as many of our camouflaged companions' senses as possible, that's vampire's blood in the air. And we deliberately leave the box out to share our secret with the macabre masses.

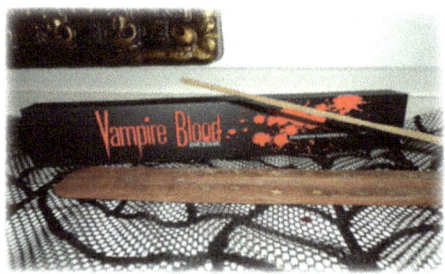

Spidery Threads—As mentioned, sporadically placed and undetectable to the naked eye, lengths of thread can be felt brushing a cheek or sliding across a hairline from time to time throughout the castle.

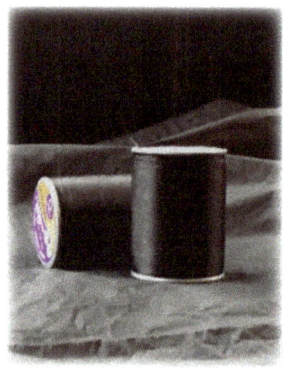

Last, we share a number of the castle's illusionary inner workings.

# Illusions

With so much going on inside the castle's walls, it's easy to miss our little arachnid friend here who drops down into the party every once in a while to get a better view of the bazaar happenings all around. Initiating his decent via a toggle switch from the other end of the room, timing is everything as he seemingly waits patiently for an unsuspecting passerby prior to venturing down from his secluded nesting place to say "hello."

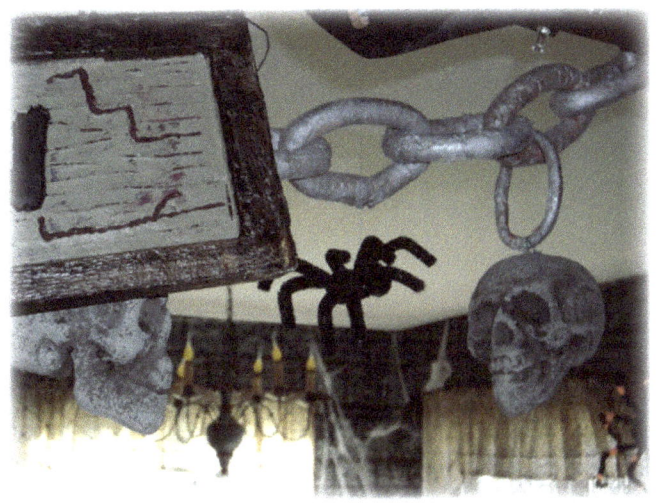

This creepy homemade critter is guaranteed to invoke more than a shriek or two as the party rocks on into the night. The spider is nothing more than black pipe cleaners wrapped around a metal bolt (to give it weight) and appropriately formed into its arachnid shape. Operating off a small motor (salvaged from an old printer), we were sure to incorporate a flattened spool as opposed to a round one as it gives the spider's decent a wobbling motion that ensures he draws the attention he deserves whenever he drops down in to visit the party. Details, details (is my OCD showing yet?). Accordingly, this little party plaything remains a favorite amongst our invited guests.

Seriously...where do we find this stuff? One of my kids gets credit for discovering this most awesome of additions to the halls of Frankenstein's Halloween playground. Downloaded from some website (just search for "dragon illusion"), this slick little 3-D illusion works on everyone, every time! Just print it out, cut along the dotted line, fold into this three-dimensional dragon shape and tape together. We printed out all of our dungeon dragons in gray to better blend with the castle's walls. Then we planted them throughout the chambers to keep an eye on things, which they do from their high perches continually with their heads seemingly rotating to follow each of our guests as they wander from party room to party room throughout the night. Just what we needed, castle watchdogs...or rather, dragons!

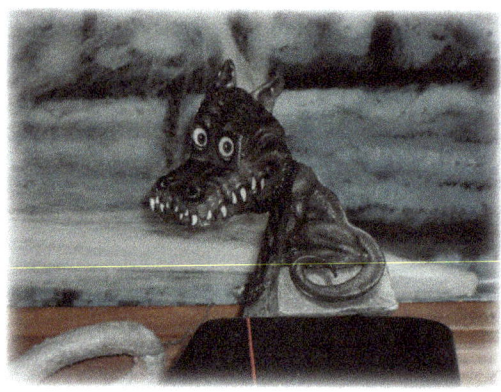

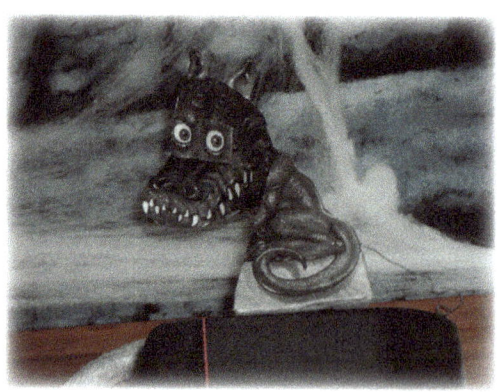

Gadgets...you gotta have 'em! The more interactive playthings you have at your party, the more entertained your horde of Halloween-goers will be. This toy illusion generator is perfectly suited for Frankenstein's castle, especially when using the most widely recognized Halloween treat for its source of deception. Just drop the candy corn (or any object of your choosing) into the disc-shaped base, and its image is regenerated as if sitting on top of the unit waiting for someone to come along and grab it. We knew our party was missing something—ghost candy!

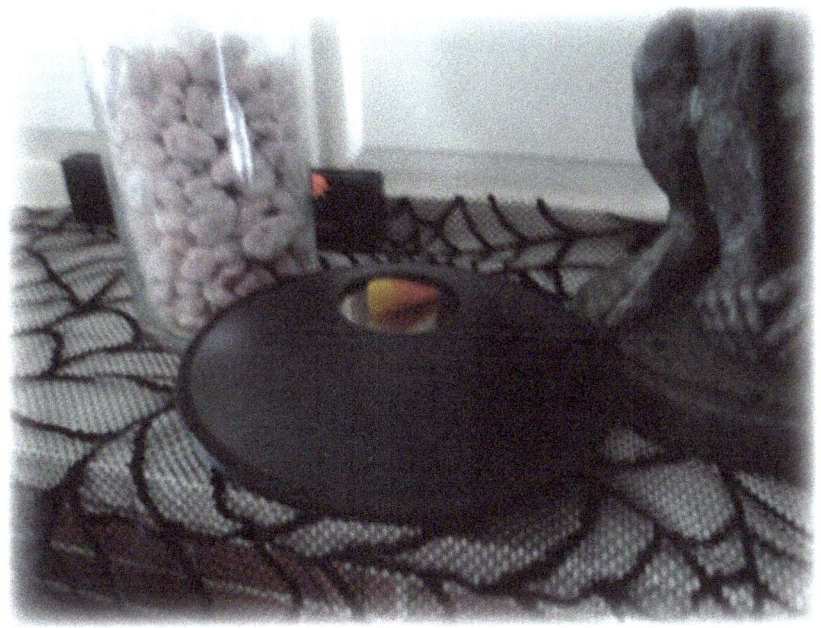

And the more illusions, the better. While one of these next store-bought "spooky" portraits remains a nice effect no matter where it's hung, here in our virtual castle, they are a MUST...serving as complimentary detail 'filler' while adding character to a number of our castle's chambers. Here, first we see "Aunt Clara" eerily transforming into a corpse as you pass by her hanging photo.

Before...

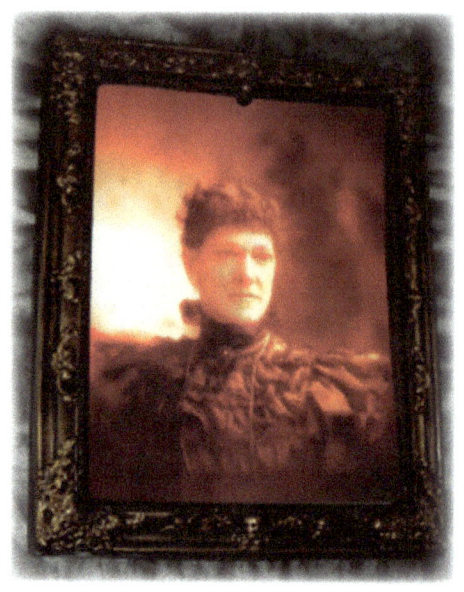

And after...

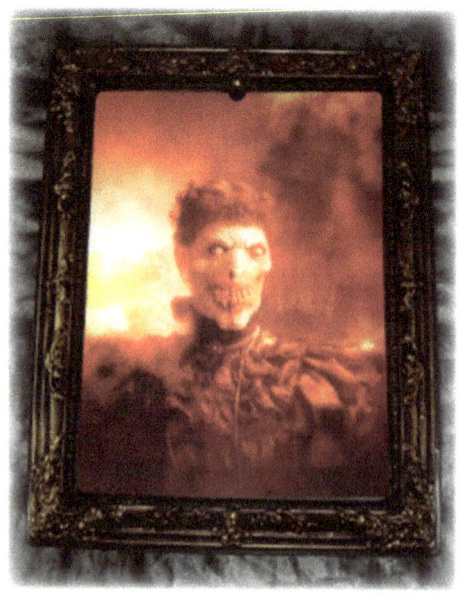

Another example, this one a family portrait.
Before...

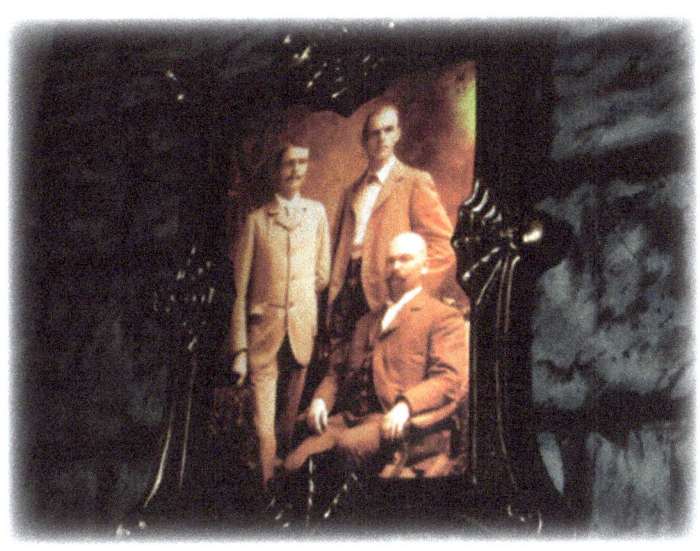

And after...

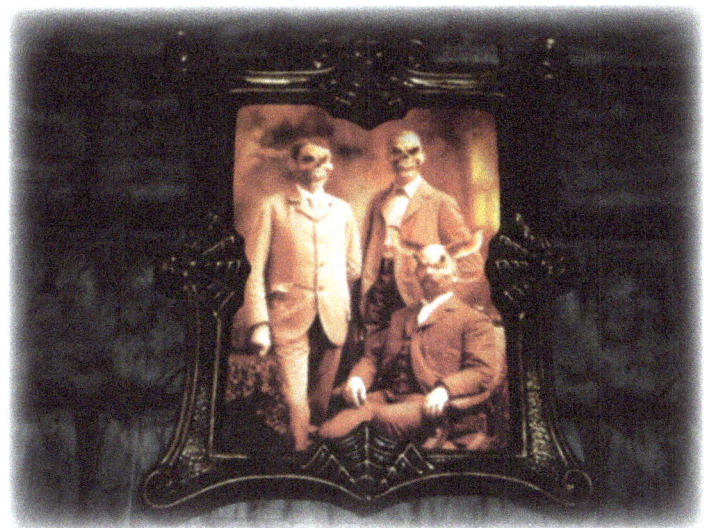

Every entrance is a grand one as new invitees get introduced to our elaborate masquerade. One by one, they pass from the outside world into our dungeon party, instantly becoming an animated castle prop dressed in whatever attire they've chosen for the evening as their senses all simultaneously come under attack. The dim lighting is tinted orange with hints of fog all about. There's an unfamiliar odor in the air, not at all unpleasant...kind of sweet but with a musky overtone. They venture further in, and the assault on their senses spreads. Eyes widen, taking in one after another of the visual oddities that are strewn throughout, occasionally brushing an errant cobweb off their face as they roam throughout their surreal surroundings. Indeed, there's a lot going on, and the deliberately poor lighting helps to blur the line between what's real and that which they are now being confronted.

With their power of sight being increasingly tested, our virtual castlelike reality is definitely well promoted as elements seemingly meld together...and defects disappear. Rubber and plastic become skin and bones; Styrofoam becomes steel. Imperfections in the wall covering blend as flame pots dance to life. While most would say they have become visually impaired, we respectfully disagree claiming our heavily Halloween-themed-party environment is just now coming into focus.

Of course, your purchases may vary greatly from the ones depicted here in these pages. Our focus is really more on the degree of detail regarding not only the items procured but how and where they're incorporated into the overall scheme of things. As such, utilization of space that otherwise goes unnoticed is an ongoing theme, as is the variety of ways we attempt to engage and entertain our costumed crowd. Toward that end, we've gone out of our way to involve each of our guests' senses through a variety of eye-catching displays, rumbling thunderstorms, spiderwebs dangling from ceilings, essence of "vampire's blood" in the air, numerous interactive playthings, and a number of taste treats we cover more extensively in our "Food/Drink" section.

Now that our virtual haunted house has "come to life," and with all of its detailed inner workings...rather exorbitantly I might add, what exactly is going to be taking place INSIDE the halls of Frankenstein's Castle?

Of course, there will be music, but what to play?

# Entertainment

## Music

Well, at THIS party, full of middle-aged crazy people who aren't quite ready to stop being stupid, nothing's going to put them in a better party mood than the "hard rock" we grew up with through the eighties, a true collection of the best hard rock songs possibly ever assembled. Talking a pretty good game here, aren't I? But can I <u>deliver</u>? The answer (after seven years, six iterations, and a heap of revision cuts left on the editing room floor) is a resounding YES!

It turns out that even in this age of computer-generated shortcuts, you can't just "dial up" the "best rock of the eighties" and expect to actually get what you're looking for...go figure. So it took me that long to search, locate, edit, and condense nearly five hours of the best hard rock music (for my money) ever put together. But don't take my word for it, take a listen for yourself! To save you the trouble of tracing my steps over the past several years, I've included the playlist here for your approval! That's right. All told, I'm giving you sixty of the best hard rock titles ever assembled to give you a jump start toward throwing your own party, Halloween or otherwise! The bottom line here is, even if you never use any of the ideas contained in these pages toward creating a grand party of your own, if you love hard rock, our castle party playlist will more than make up for the cost of this book. So jump on iTunes, download them onto a set of CDs, and enjoy at your own leisure! Without further ado, our predominantly eighties themed playlist...

"Don't Fear the Reaper" ...................................................Blue Öyster Cult

"Rocket" ...................................................Def Leppard

"Giving the Dog a Bone" ...................................................AC/DC

"Mama We're All Crazee Now" ...................................................Quiet Riot

"N.I.B." ...................................................Black Sabbath

"Nothing but a Good Time" ...................................................Poison

"Cherry Pie" ...................................................Warrant

"Kickstart My Heart" ...................................................Mötley Crüe

"Hells Bells" ...................................................AC/DC

"You've Got Another Thing Comin'" ...................................................Judas Priest

"Slow Ride" ...................................................Foghat

"Same Ol' Situation" ...................................................Mötley Crüe

"Never Been Any Reason" ...................................................Head East

"I Don't Wanna Stop" ...................................................Ozzy Osbourne

"Werewolves of London" ...................................................Warren Zevon

"Dr. Feelgood" ...................................................Mötley Crüe

"Balls to the Wall" ...................................................Accept

"Round and Round" ...................................................Ratt

"American Woman" ...................................................Lenny Kravitz

"Shot in the Dark" ...................................................Ozzy Osbourne

"Thriller" ...................................................Michael Jackson

"Loving Every Minute of It" ...................................................Loverboy

"Girls, Girls, Girls" ...................................................Mötley Crüe

"Symphony of Destruction" ...................................................Megadeth

"Wild Thing" ...................................................Sam Kinison

"Lick It Up" ...................................................Kiss

"Living Dead Thing" ...................................................Rob Zombie

"I Don't Know" ...................................................Ozzy Osbourne

"Cult of Personality" ...................................................Living Colour

"Mr. Crowley" ...................................................Ozzy Osbourne

"She Goes Down" ...................................................Mötley Crüe

"Never Say Goodbye" ...................................................................Bon Jovi

"American Witch" ...................................................................Rob Zombie

"The Zoo" ...................................................................Scorpions

"Too Much Time on My Hands" ...................................................................Styx

"No More Tears" ...................................................................Ozzy Osbourne

"Still Born" ...................................................................Black Label Society

"Black Sabbath" ...................................................................Black Sabbath

"Feed My Frankenstein" ...................................................................Alice Cooper

"Unskinny Bop" ...................................................................Poison

"Get Down, Make Love" ...................................................................Queen

"Closer" ...................................................................Nine Inch Nails

"Jailbreak" ...................................................................Thin Lizzy

"Still Loving You" ...................................................................Scorpions

"Monster Mash" ...................................................................Bobby Pickett/The Crypt-Kickers

"Too Late for Love" ...................................................................Def Leppard

"Fat Bottomed Girls" ...................................................................Queen

"Man in the Box" ...................................................................Alice in Chains

"Lord of Your Thighs" ...................................................................Aerosmith

"Turn Up the Radio" ...................................................................Autograph

"Up All Night" ...................................................................Slaughter

"Slow an' Easy" ...................................................................Whitesnake

"D.O.A." ...................................................................Bloodrock

"Wait for You" ...................................................................Bonham

"Heaven and Hell" ...................................................................Black Sabbath

"Strut" ...................................................................Bob Seger

"I Drink Alone" ...................................................................George Thorogood

"Animal" ...................................................................Def Leppard

"War Pigs" ...................................................................Black Sabbath

"Detroit Rock City" ...................................................................Kiss

Not only was this playlist created over a seven-year period, but as implied, it too has "evolved." This Halloween production (and I use the word *production* because on many levels, this party is just as much theatrical as anything else) has a flow to it. At the beginning, the "meet and greet" occurs with our invited guests mingling, investigating the castle's decor, checking out everyone else's costume, seeing what's on the menu, and perhaps getting that first "refreshment" in their hand, etc. This sort of "start-up" activity takes place over the first hour or so while all the ghouls and goblins assemble. Then there's the middle where the party begins in earnest, really takes hold and continues on into the night, until around the last hour or so when all our wannabe trick-or-treaters finally start to filter out (the "wind down"). It's no coincidence that by design, the playlist for our ghostly get-togethers is a reflection of this dynamic with the "best of the best" selections starting to ramp up as that first hour of "orientation" passes, steadily adding intensity until it reaches another level ("best of the best of the best") which it maintains throughout the bulk of the party before winding down toward the end of the night.

For me, the height of the soundtrack culminates with Black Sabbath playing its namesake, "Black Sabbath." Although there's loads of great music both before and after, to me, that song proves to be most appropriate in our mocked-up dungeon setting. (This is usually one of the times during the night that I take a moment to step back and soak in our castle party with all its contents, inhabitants, and all. I find great pleasure in being witness to all our friends having such a good time and knowing that I had something to do with it...making my prep time investment well worth the effort.) Finally, the music settles back down to what I simply call "solid" hard rock tunes as the party grinds down to its inevitable conclusion.

But my absolute favorites are crunched into the peak hours of the party. It's during that middle portion of our Halloween bash that all remaining demons get exorcised from any attendee who wasn't quite sure if this was the party for them (as they may have been dragged "kicking and screaming" by their partner from the onset to get into a costume and make an appearance for the sake of the relationship). But when the party really starts to rock, there's something for everyone...with most offerings stirring up fond memories of days gone by or, better still, tapping into something much more primitive, drilling down right to the core, the very essence of your being. While everyone's taste is different, it's impossible not to feel the excitement in the dungeon air when Frankenstein's Castle party really gets under way. In the end, not only do we boast an awesome collection of music, geared for a six-hour event, but the individual songs have been meticulously arranged such that they help DRIVE the very "life" of the party! No matter the theme of your party soundtrack, we highly recommend a similar approach.

You'll also notice that there are a number of specific Halloween-related selections mixed in throughout the "meat" of the playlist such as Alice Cooper's "Feed My Frankenstein," Michael Jackson's "Thriller," Bob Pickett and the Crypt Kickers' "Monster Mash," Bloodrock's "D.O.A.," Warren Zevon's "Werewolves of London," and Rob Zombie's "American Witch."

What you don't see on the list is the more detailed "customization," the additional Halloween-themed throw-ins in between every couple of songs that appear on the actual party soundtrack. Appropriately placed are dozens of horrifically delicious sound bites, such as snippets of castle organ music, witch cackles, monster screams, wolf howls, creaky doors, heartbeats, and one of my favorites, Vincent Price's evil laugh at the end of Michael Jackson's "Thriller," to name a few.

Along with these ten-to-fifteen-second segments of themed audio, we've also incorporated more lengthy portions of sound bites from classic horror films such as the piano music from *Halloween*, theme music from *Psycho*, *The Omen*, *Sinister Street*, *Torment*, etc., and a little something entitled "Fires of Hell" derived from a "Halloween Spooky Sound Effects" CD among others. Once inter-dispersed with our playlist, the audio soundtrack stretches approximately five hours of music out to six hours of uninterrupted entertainment (with game time organ music also adding significantly to the overall length of available audio).

As mentioned, additional audio effects include a booming thunderstorm that remain part of the castle's atmosphere throughout the entirety of the evening played on a separate surround sound system in our virtual dungeon party room. And it can't be overstated enough that we switch CDs on the house stereo system when it comes time to play any one of our castle specialty games for our invited guests. When it's game time, our eighties-hard rock-theme music changes to "haunted castle" appropriate organ music, specifically "Toccata in D minor," Frankenstein's favorite! Against the backdrop of our virtual thunderstorm, the stage becomes ever so awesomely set for our dungeon room contests. Speaking of Halloween games, what might we be talking about here? Let's take a closer look, shall we?

Okay, so the party's in full swing, now what? What do you do with a bunch of silly grown-ups acting like kids...role playing (nonetheless) in this most ultimate of virtual playgrounds now that you've got them all here? Simple. We emphasize the silly! And that's exactly what we kept in mind while creating the following list of activities to periodically subject our visitors to throughout Frankenstein's Castle party. So please step into the dungeon where we'll begin your initiation toward instilling yet more life into our ghostly gala on this most grand of nights.

## Games

As you can see reading down through the following list, we've come up with some pretty creative contests in an effort to appropriately complement our somewhat elaborate Halloween get-togethers. Also, if your event is anything like ours, you'll want to have as little to do the day of the party as possible, so to help promote a calamity free evening, we've included some helpful hints for prepping each game.

Now without further ado, on a scale of 1–5 skulls (with a 5 monstrously delivering the goods), they go something like this:

# Candy Corn Suck
## (Rating: 4 skulls)

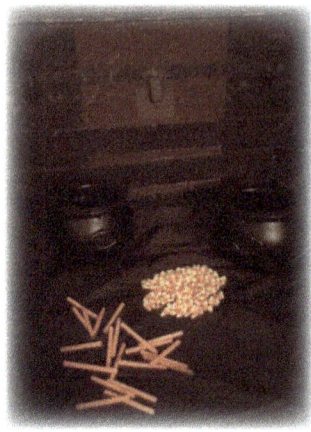

A personal favorite for its simplicity, as well as visual appeal. This game is easy to set up, easy to explain, and fun to watch. First, we break the group up into two teams (guys versus girls has always worked well for us). At one end of our dungeon, we place two chairs with a pile of candy corn spread out on each. At the other end of the room, we place two more chairs, each holding an empty cauldron. The teams form two separate lines, one behind each pile of candy corn with every individual armed with a three-to-four inch long straw ("fatter" straws work better than skinny ones). When the game begins, the first person in each line leans over, straw in mouth, sucks up a candy corn (sticking it to the opposite end of the straw) and without assistance from any external source walks the length of the room and deposits their candy corn into their teams waiting cauldron using nothing but suction power. The next contestant cannot begin their turn until the previous person has delivered their candy corn into the cauldron. Personally, I don't have any trouble picking up a candy corn this way and walking around with it stuck to the end of a straw, which makes it all the more curious as to why some people are all but incapable of performing this seemingly simple task. Some make it all the way on the first try; others make it halfway before dropping it, causing them to start over with a new candy corn; but some just cannot pick up the candy at all. It was for those few that we made a new rule—after one or more attempts, you can forfeit your turn and take a time penalty (make one up). If the teams have equal numbers, the first team to finish, wins (minus any time penalty). Note: For longer games, go through the line more than once. If splitting the group into male/female doesn't even up the teams, either make a quick fix or use a time limit instead and count the number of candy corns in each cauldron at the end. My wife and I "emcee" each event, but if there ends up being an odd number of contestants, one of us can always jump in to even up the teams.

## Game Prep

- Requires little. Just make sure you have the straws precut into three-to-four-inch lengths, and there are plenty to go around. Remember, fat straws work much better than skinny ones.
- A large bag of candy corn and two cauldrons later and you're ready to go.

## Mummy Wrap
## (Rating: 3 skulls)

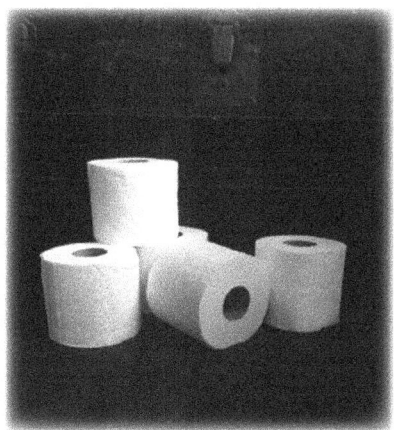

For this game, separate the group into teams of three each. Each team will have to have one of its members' volunteer to be the "mummy." You will also need to purchase a number of rolls of toilet paper...enough to supply each team with one roll. Through trial and error, we will warn you outright not to buy the cheap stuff as the goal of this game is to wrap your "mummy" in toilet paper in one continuous sheet until the paper roll is empty. (For longer games, you can unroll your mummy prior to claiming victory). Hint: If you don't want to get anyone dizzy, the best approach is to have one of the people in charge of the "rolling" on one side of your mummy and one on the other side. The roll of paper can be handed back and forth as they wrap (instead of having to run around and around the mummy). Just be sure to purchase triple-ply, extra strength paper for best results. This game is well themed and fun but is best suited for smaller party groups as space to perform this task, at some point, may be an issue—not to mention monitoring everyone's progress.

## Game Prep

- Procuring a sufficient number of <u>extra-strength</u> rolls of toilet paper is all that is required.
- Give some thought as to how you're going to utilize your available space to pull this game off as it does require an ample amount. As such, this game is recommended for smaller crowds.

## Scavenger Hunt
### (Rating: 5 skulls)

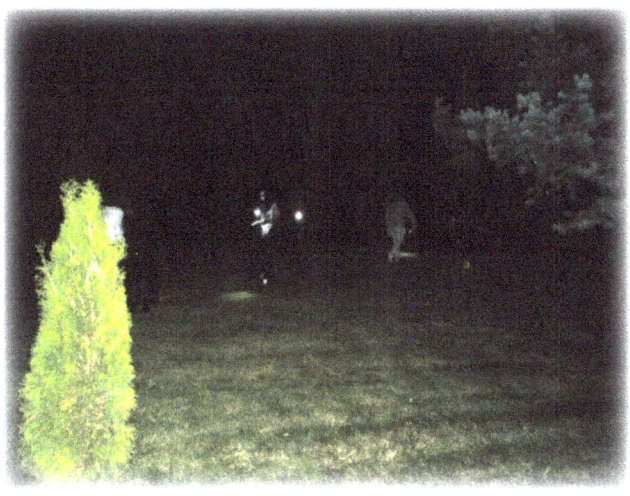

The ultimate in Halloween party games, if for no other reason, because it's played outdoors in the pitch-black with a bunch of costumed morons trouncing around with apparent purpose. This one scores a ten on both the fun, as well as the visually appealing scales. However, you do need good weather and a decently sized yard also helps. In our case, we include ours, as well as the neighbor's backyard as the "playing field." (Note: we ask in our invitations for each guest to bring a flashlight. We also have a small collection of them stockpiled at home for anyone who forgets). In our version, we split the teams up into a number of groups, four to a group. For the sake of this explanation, let's say you had twenty guests. With four in each group, there would be five groups. We purchased twelve plastic cauldrons and placed five identical items in each—five eyeballs in one, five bats in another, five skulls in another, etc.

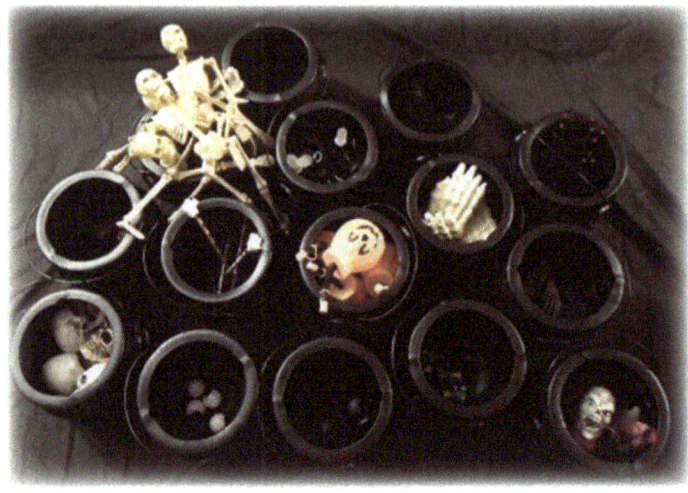

Then we spread them out in plain sight across the playing field. We then create five complete lists of the items that are in the cauldrons—eyeball, bat, skull, etc. Tear each list into four pieces with three items on each of the pieces. Hand the smaller lists out to the individual members of each team so that every individual is responsible for finding three items on their teams list (of twelve total items). Mark off a "home base." Get ready...get set... GO! Out into the darkness, they rush, guided only by their flashlights. The first team to regroup having gathered all the items together at "home base" (and has their list verified), wins! Only a couple of rules: (1) contestants can only pick up the items that appear on their individual lists (and only ONE of them) and (2) no traveling in groups. We once had a whole team move around together to every cauldron, ensuring that they were collecting one of everything methodically moving through the playing field. It's much more fun watching them running randomly around, avoiding each other, screaming in delight whenever they find what they're after, not to mention the "hauntingly" spooky scene it creates for anyone watching. This one's a definite "keeper."

## Game Prep

- Divide all scavenger hunt items by type and place each group of them into separate cauldrons. The cauldron's can then be scattered around the playing field at your convenience prior to the start of the party. Note: Try to spread the items out such that they do not show up out on the playing field as they appear on the list (next to each other).

- Create a number of complete lists of the items to be collected by each team. This list should include one of every item in the playing field. Once the number of members in each team has been determined, cut each list up such that every player has as close to the same number of items to find as possible. Repeat as necessary for each team.

- Just prior to game time, ensure that everyone has a flashlight (keep extras on hand for those who forgot to bring one).

- Have them gather outside before attempting to explain the rules of engagement. It's easier to gain (and maintain) everyone's attention, and there's a little more explaining to do regarding this particular competition with lists being passed out, etc.

# Witches Brew (with Mummy Hands)
## (Rating: 4 skulls)

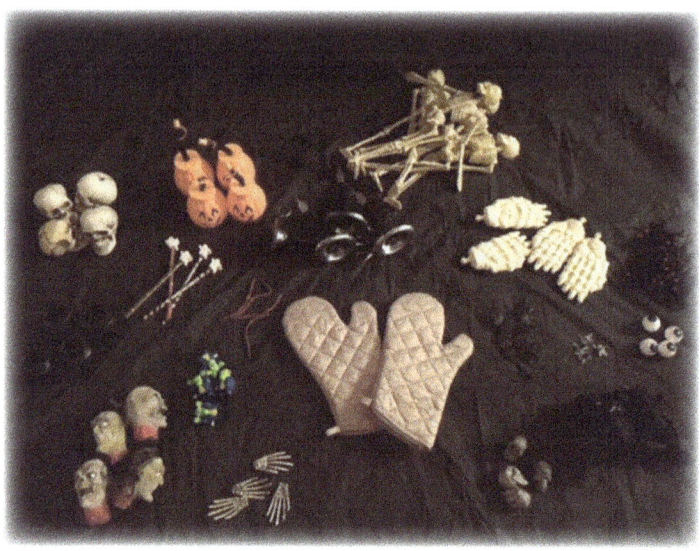

This game was created one year when the weather outside did not allow for our scavenger hunt to take place. Instead, we put the items purchased for the hunt to good use by making them the ingredients in our "witches brew." This contest is creative, always proves to get the crowd excited, and well themed.

First, split the group into two teams (again, we find that dividing up girls versus guys makes for better bonding/competition in any game). At one end of our dungeon, we place a large plastic tub filled with the items purchased for the scavenger hunt, all mixed together. At the opposite end of the room, we place two large empty cauldrons. The lists of the items for the witches brew are cut up into single, individual "ingredients," folded and placed into two separate piles (one pile for each team) near the starting line. Each team forms a line extending from either side of the tub and is given one pair of oven mitts (mummy hands). When the game begins, the first person in each line picks a piece of paper revealing the ingredient they are to add to the "witches brew," puts on the "mummy hands," and dives into the tub in search of the item on the paper they chose. The mummy hands not only ensure more of a "relay" feel to this game but add an extra degree of difficulty, especially when picking up certain "ingredients" (i.e. small gravestones are easy... eyeballs, not so much). Once the ingredient has been picked up and delivered down into the waiting cauldron, the first person runs back and passes the mummy hands off to the next person in line, who then chooses an ingredient from the pile and puts on the mummy hands, etc. As long as everyone at the party gets at least one turn, then everybody's happy. Ideally, if you had twelve different ingredients and twenty-four guests (twelve in each line), if you go once through the line (and ingredients), you will have satisfied all requirements and, generally speaking, have created a long enough contest to call it complete. Of course you can always go through the line twice, or if you have thirty people, the first three can go again, or no matter how many people are playing, add another degree of difficulty by having each person find and deliver two of whatever ingredient they have chosen, etc. Adjust as you see fit.

## Game Prep

- Should foul weather cause you to abort the scavenger hunt (if one had been planned), take the ingredients for the witches' brew (the items from the scavenger hunt) and place them all in a large plastic tub.
- Keeping everything you'll need together, also throw in two pairs of mummy hands (oven mitts) and two decent-sized cauldrons, one for each team to create their witches brew in.

# Eyeballs in the Skull Head
## (Rating: 4 skulls)

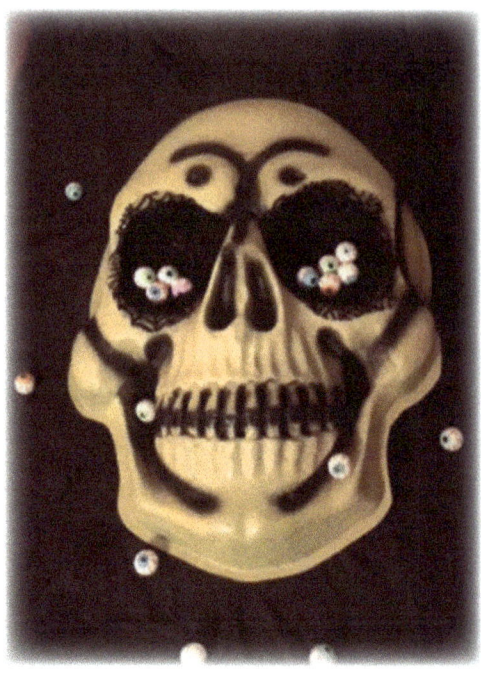

A perfect example of creating something out of nothing...this "home-made" game was developed using whatever was available while maintaining our Halloween party theme. It's another easy to set up/easy to explain contest that underscores the silliness of the overall occasion. One of the props we had purchased years prior was a giant skeleton face that is designed to hang on a wall approximately three and a half feet tall with large sunken features in it. (Note: We've come across this same item in numerous stores over the years.)

We bought a stockpile of ping-pong balls and spent one afternoon coloring them to resemble bloodshot eyeballs. What we do is lay the giant skull face on the (hard) kitchen floor, a short distance from the carpeted dungeon area where we form our guests into two teams. The object is to bounce an eyeball into the eye socket on your team's side of the skull face. It's surprising how many eyeballs fit into one of those big eye sockets—fifteen or more. The trick is to get the first eyeball to stay in the socket. The skeleton face is made of hard plastic and, as such, possesses "deflective" properties. So much so, that we slightly "deadened" (again, pun intended) each socket by lining (gluing) black lace into them to soften the landing for the bouncing eyeballs.

Once the first one "sticks" in the socket, subsequent eyeballs have a much better chance of sticking also as they now have something other than the hard plastic to soften their landing. Set a time limit and the team with the most eyeballs in their eye socket, wins. (Note: my wife and I act as eyeball return "specialists" for this event, positioning ourselves on either side of the target area behind the giant skull face and continually sweep any eyeballs that miss their target back to the carpeted area where the lines are formed.)

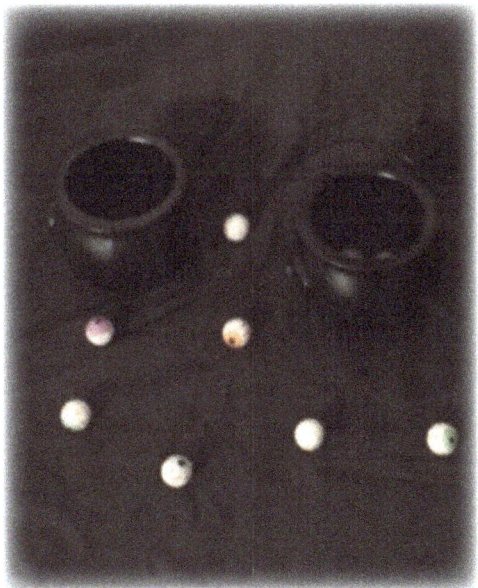

A simple variation on the theme (should a giant skull head not be available) could involve the use of a couple of cauldrons, perhaps half filled with water and subsequently be called "eyeball stew."

## Game Prep

- Paint/color (permanent markers work best) two to three dozen ping-pong balls to look like bloodshot eyeballs and keep them together with the giant skull head. Note: While an oversized skull head has a certain allure to it, if one cannot be procured, two cauldrons will work fine in a pinch.

- If necessary, deaden the eye sockets of your skull head by gluing some black lace or black cloth material into each one to help the eyeballs settle into the sockets. Experiment beforehand by attempting to land (bounce) a ping-pong ball into the eye sockets and getting them to rest there, adding more material accordingly. The trick is getting the first one to stay. Those that follow will then have something to deaden their landing, increasing the odds that accurate bounces will be rewarded.

## Apple "Bobbing"
### (Rating: 3 skulls)

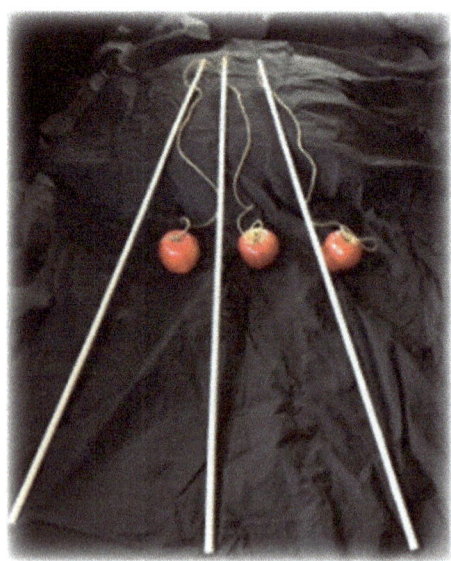

Since bobbing for apples seems to be historically linked to Halloween parties, we introduced the concept of "dry" apple bobbing at one of our first get-togethers. Our version goes like this: We gather a number of sticks to act as "fishing rods" and tie a two-to-three-foot length of string to the end of each stick. To the opposite end of each string, we tie an apple. This contest has each of the couples we invite to the party pitted against one another as one of them holds the fishing rod and "fishes" for their mate by trying to get them to sink their teeth into the dangling apple presented in front of their face—no hands allowed. This was initially more difficult than we anticipated. Anyone who has ever bobbed for apples in a bucket of water can attest to the fact that there is very little chance that you can bite into one without submerging at least part of your face/head into the water so you can press the apple against the side of the bucket in order to sink your teeth into it. However, when the apple is suspended in midair, there is nothing against which you can press the apple to gain any leverage. The answer, of course, is to use smaller apples for our "dry" version. The secret is to experiment beforehand and find appropriately sized apples for your game. Nonetheless, this is still a pretty entertaining contest, especially for smaller groups.

## Game Prep

- Appropriately sized apples are key here. You'll have to experiment by purchasing two to three different sizes and attempting to "apple bob" on your own to determine which size works best. Be sure to buy apples with the stem intact (to attach the string).
- Fashion some "fishing poles" out of whatever…you may have some garden stakes lying around, you can purchase wooden dowels at a home improvement center or simply go into the woods and pick out some workable sticks of adequate length.

- Tie a string (approximately two feet in length) to one end of each pole. Attach an apple to the opposite end of each string and you're ready to go.

## Raising the Dead
### (Rating: 4 skulls)

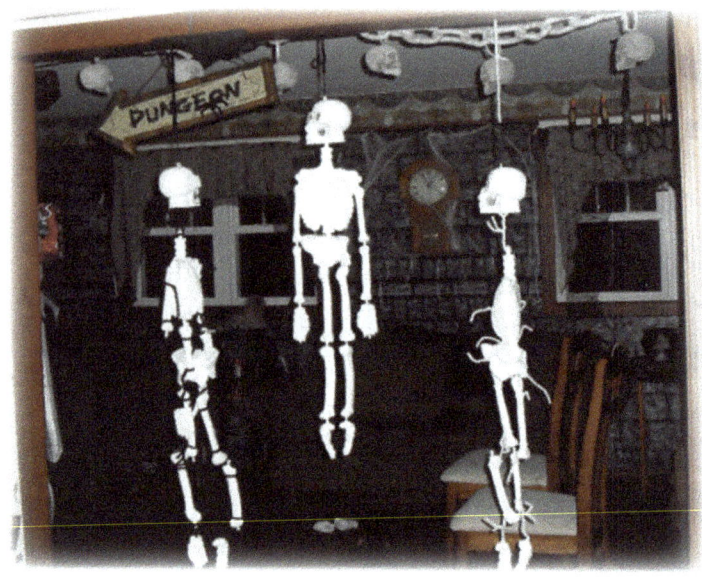

Suitably named, this contest involves the reconstruction of a skeleton, bone by bone. Luckily our house boasts the perfect place to perform this event as there is a double-wide entranceway between our centrally located kitchen and the dungeon (game room). It is in this opening that we secure three small hooks to the overhead frame from which our skeletons get "raised from the dead." You will need to purchase three medium-sized (three-foot tallish/hollow plastic), break-apart skeletons and two packages of different colored pipe cleaners. We incorporate the use of pipe cleaners to color code each complete set of bones, slow the pace of the game, and promote artistic license (the three-foot skeleton will most likely be closer to four-to-five feet when complete).

First, disassemble two of the skeletons, keeping each complete set of bones segregated. Attach one end of a pipe cleaner to each end of every bone, leaving enough excess to allow for a twisted connection to be made to the next bone to be attached. Each bone will have a male, as well as a female end when they come out of the package. While you can probably wrap/twist a pipe cleaner securely enough to the male end, you might have to poke an extra hole in the female end of each bone and thread the pipe cleaner through to appropriately secure it. We jokingly warn competitors that they will lose "style points" in the event of a close finish should they not reassemble to "original specifications."

As a guide for our guests to refer to, we hang a third skeleton (in its original form) from the center hook in between where each team will attempt to be the first to "raise their skeleton from the dead." Before the game, we pre-attach the first bone of each team's skeleton (the skull) to a length of pipe cleaner hanging from each of their respective hooks. We then place the two complete sets of bones a distance away from where they will be "raised from the dead" and form two lines behind them…girls versus guys as usual. (Hosts note: any guest who comes dressed in "drag" may be placed in the opposite line at your discretion). When the game begins, the first person takes the next bone to be assembled (collarbone), brings it over to their partially assembled skeleton, and attaches it by twisting the provided pipe cleaner ends together.

Once accomplished, the second person in line locates the next appropriate bone to attach to the previous one (using the sample skeleton as a guide), etc. The first team to complete their skeleton, wins. You'll be surprised how many bones actually go into the creation of one of these skeletons—the skull, collarbone, sternum, pelvis, four leg bones, four arm bones (confusingly similar to leg bones, only shorter), two feet and two hands, ensuring everyone gets a turn.

For larger crowds, add additional skeletons and teams (or after assembling, take the skeleton apart piece by piece). Note: This game can also be played using "mummy hands" (oven mitts) to add a degree of difficulty.

## Game Prep

- Verify the bones. Make sure you have a complete set of bones for each required setup.
- Verify the attachments. Make sure that each and every bone to be assembled has a pipe cleaner securely attached at <u>each</u> end. You don't want to get into the middle of a game to find out that one skeleton has been shortchanged.
- Have the necessary hooks pre-attached to the ceiling, frame, or wherever the activity is to take place.

Additional comments:

- So now you're ready, but first, for any of the games to be played you have to get the attention of your guests. I only bring this up because they will inevitably be spread out all over the "castle," whooping it up and carrying on, and we've found that getting their attention as a group can take a little doing. So when it's game time, we do a couple of things just prior to any related announcement. First, while the thunderstorm is allowed to continue, the house music gets switched from eighties rock to our customized haunted house organ music. And believe me when I say that this little changeup (especially against the backdrop of our virtual thunderstorm) has a definite effect on the overall ambiance of our castle setting. Note: the music disc we use at game time has multiple copies of Toccata strung together to ensure there isn't a break in the audio no matter the length of the game. The other thing we do preemptively is either wildly clang a cowbell or sound off a foghorn. Doesn't matter which—they both get the job done. Only after all have gathered to within shouting distance should the rules of any chosen game be read aloud/explained. Then (and only then), we announce the commencement of a game time event as these are all-inclusive competitions and require as attentive a group as manageable.

- Space the games. It's plenty dark enough come 7:00 p.m. in late October (at least up here in the northeast) to start your party. The graveyard (or whatever display you've arranged out front on your property) will look great by then. So why waste good party time? Start your event as soon as it gets dark. Once the guests have all arrived, you'll begin to get the feel of the tempo of what's happening all around you. We suggest once the preliminary "getting acquainted" portion of the evening starts to take a back seat and you feel a slight "sag" in the entertainment level… you might just want to break the ice by dragging out the first of the nights competitions, providing a little taste of what's in store for them. We like to space the games out to about one every one and a half hour, usually getting in three games of our choosing by the end of the night. Note: Be sure to refer to the ratings in the "Games" section to see which ones our guests seem to get the biggest kick out of.

- Be sure to organize each game by segregating all of the parts involved and either bagging them up or compiling the elements in a large cauldron, etc. To avoid added confusion, we suggest you keep all the games together in a single location. We use one of the kids' bedrooms to keep them hidden until it's time to drag one out and have at it.

- Oh yeah, one last thing I should probably mention, in case you didn't know, people cheat. When they do (and they will), the judge's word is final. As the host, you are that judge. Just keep in mind that we're having fun here. And no matter what any one individual does to get around whatever rules may be in place, take it in stride and award prizes in the spirit of the game however you can best decide who the winner should be. Just be ready to have to make a decision at some point in your night of ghostly competitions.

- Finally, you can't have a party, play games that produce winners, and not have prizes. For getting involved in the spirit of the party, allowing their competitive side to emerge, and coming out victorious in between segments of pure party time, the winners will (no doubt) need to have their egos massaged with some sort of symbolic bragging right/ritualistic offering. Accordingly, we submit the following.

## Prizes

Of course, no Halloween party of any substance has ever been thrown without awarding a prize for "best costume," and this bash is no exception. Somehow this particular prize has always been associated with an actual trophy, and we agree. So starting with the first Halloween party we ever threw, we have always awarded the obligatory "best costume" trophy, in this case, a standing skeleton holding his head (plastic and purchased at any Halloween themed or even general party store). And should you choose this route but care to elaborate a bit, you can always visit your local trophy shop and either purchase a more grand-looking trophy off the shelf or work with the proprietor to customize one better to your liking. However, while winning something tangible that can be placed on the mantle at home satisfies the "bragging rights" angle, we have over the course of time also managed to 'sweeten the pot' regarding our party's best costume prize. This activity culminated in the ultimate in party prize giveaways, and justly so as costumed guests are what this party's all about! But I'm not about to tip my hand just yet. Read on.

In the beginning, the search for appropriate game prizes was seen as somewhat of an issue. Most of our contests were predicated on splitting the crowd into two groups which dictated that half of our costumed participants would be expecting an award of some kind each time we held a competition. Since we usually schedule three games during the course of a party, dozens of prizes are required to satisfy the masses. The only reasonable response was to keep the cost of the prize awards down by initially purchasing Halloween-themed necklace medallions (a dozen per package) for a couple of bucks each.

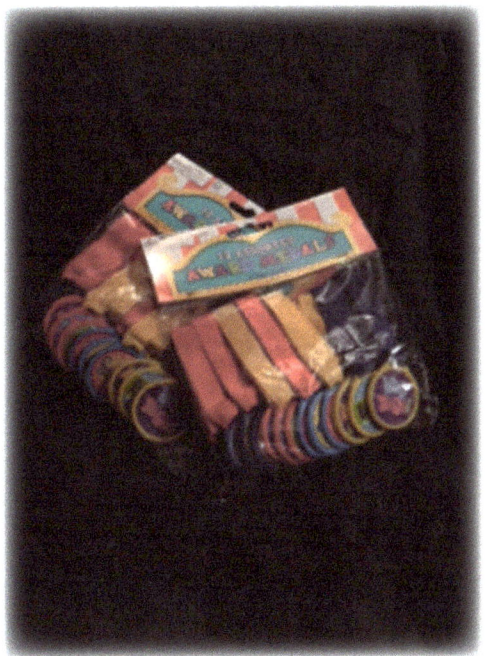

But then a funny thing happened. We handed the necklaces out to the first winners to receive them, and the medallions instantly turned into a "badge of honor" allowing them to proudly display their symbolic bragging rights around their neck for all to see (not to mention the verbal barrage aimed at the not-so-fortunate "second-place finishers" that ensued in the aftermath). The medallions also served to heat up future competitions. After all, one could accumulate multiple necklaces over the course of the night while some may not get a single one, so in the end, not only were they cheap to procure but the crowd ate them up!

However, the game prizes couldn't be left behind as the party continued to evolve through the years. But how were we supposed to improve upon them without going broke? And then...a stroke of genius! It was perfect! And best of all, we already <u>had</u> it. The MUSIC! We knew the party soundtrack was a huge hit with this crowd, so we created a customized Halloween party CD and appropriately called it "Dungeon Rock—The Best of the Best of the Best." We even designed a cover for it...a picture of the inside of an authentic medieval dungeon, complete with torches mounted on stonewalls. I hand selected the best fifteen songs (to my taste) from the "meat" of our Halloween party soundtrack, bought a package of blank CDs and cases, and created the perfect prize giveaway for our partygoers...a prize actually WORTH something, and they absolutely <u>loved</u> it!

Always attempting to outdo ourselves, the following year, we generated the sequel, "Dungeon Rock—The Best of the <u>Rest.</u>" Of course we had to create a brand-new cover and did so by displaying an antiquated picture of closed dungeon doors on the "jacket." For anyone who had already received the original CD the previous year, we handed out the second-generation CD while "newbies" received the original.

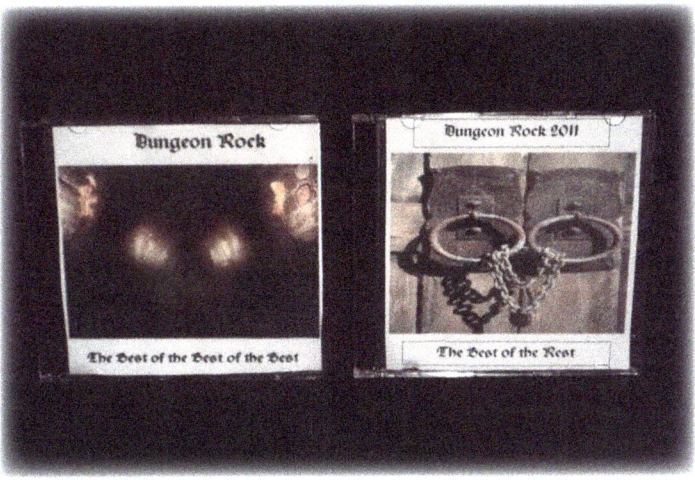

By the way, so as not to take away bragging rights (as well as dealing with the issue of what to do with a CD while you're partying down), we still gave out the medallions as a place holder for the CD to be collected on the way out as a "part(y)ing gift." As mentioned, many guests end up with a number of medallions by the end of the party (only one CD per customer please), but with the splitting up of the teams, playing multiple games ensures that every household represented at the party goes home a "winner."

And oh yeah, I almost forgot...so what about the best costume winner? On top of the customary first-place trophy, that lucky individual now receives the complete Halloween party soundtrack, all five CDs worth, making us quite possibly the best party hosts on the entire planet!

Pure genius...

# Food/Drink

Although food is not the central focus of the party, it certainly lends itself nicely toward infusing ever more themed detail into the event. That and it IS a <u>party</u>, so you should definitely have something to nibble on for those in need. Accordingly, while it's a foregone conclusion that (as the host) you should indeed provide the "necessities," we stress that you should look outward toward your invited guests to provide significant assistance when it comes to filling your feast table. As a matter of fact, many consider it a welcome challenge to come up with as creative a recipe as possible to help dress up the appearance of the offerings, so much so there are always a number of surprises showing up to complement the existing spread.

So first things first, ask people to bring something to eat (and be sure to mention the Halloween theme). That said, we always ensure that there's something of substance available for those requiring it, so here's where I should at least mention spiral ham! It doesn't take a lot of fuss and certainly makes for an ideal centerpiece on the table while tying in nicely with our roasted wild boar theme (if anyone asks). All you're really doing is heating the thing up at low temperature, maybe slapping a glaze on it and serve. It's tasty, filling, and looks great centrally placed amongst whatever else gets conjured up.

Crock pots are a good use of table space as well. Of course, if real estate is an issue, they can always be left on the kitchen counter, plugged in and full of any one of a number of simple, yet tasty treats such as cocktail franks in sweet-and-sour sauce, Swedish meatballs, etc. We always have a couple of them going, each holding a little something different. My wife

88

also usually gets up enough ambition to heat up a couple of large bags of honey-flavored chicken wings (bats wings...if anyone asks) on some cookie sheets and adds them to the food spread some time mid-party to keep the taste buds satisfied, although I say that's going above and beyond.

Needless to say, nearly everything we serve is Halloween themed, whether it be through the name alone as mentioned above or via a more deliberate approach focused mainly on creative presentation. While candy corn, devil dogs, deviled eggs, pumpkin pie (or pumpkin anything), etc. are never out of place, once we get past the subtly obvious, we tend to get somewhat carried away, and little by little, we (with an assist from our guests) make Frankenstein's banquet more of a full-blown production. Some favorites that have graced our haunted castle's feast table over the years include the following:

## Assorted Munchies

### Finger food

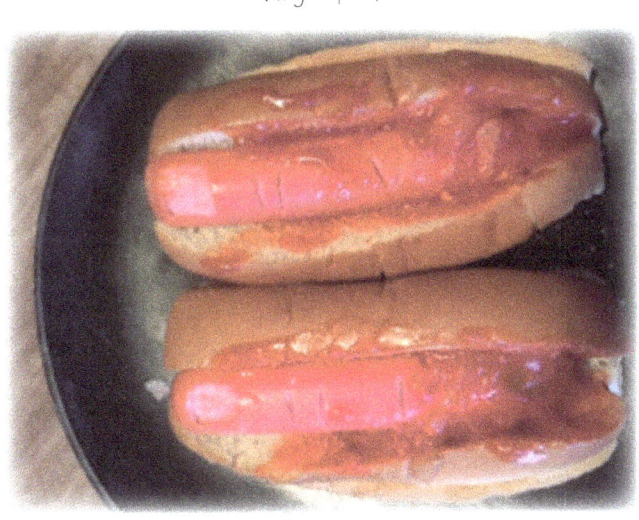

Don't know who thinks this stuff up but how morbidly appropriate!

Another variation on the theme...still creative in a demented sort of way, but oddly enough, speaks to one's taste buds in a tad more of an enticing manner.

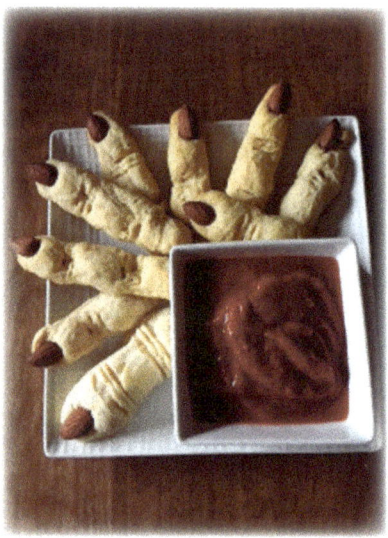

Our sincere thanks goes out to those who have supplied each and every interpretation we've been served over time on this subject matter. Seemingly, some of our sicker acquaintances have clearly lopped off more than many discriminating others dare to chew.

Mummy Dogs

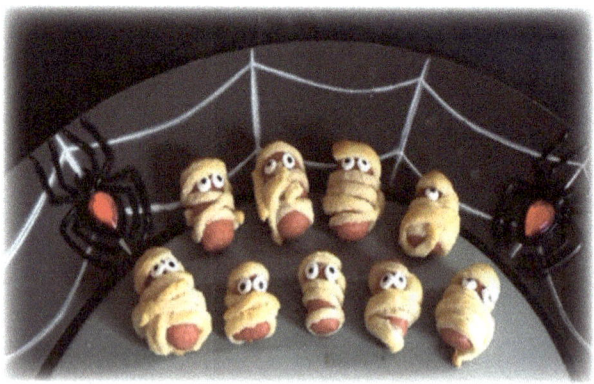

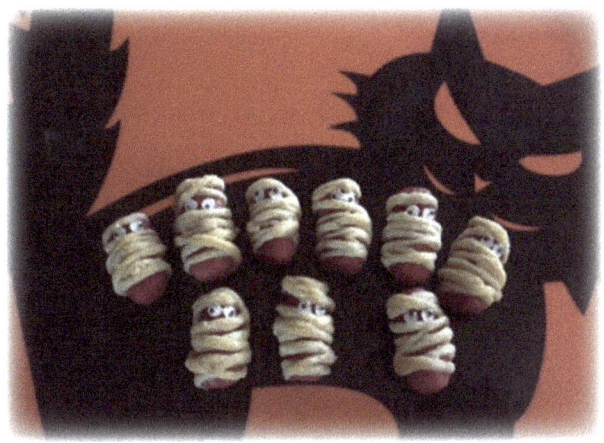

These guys are both tasty and just plain fun with no two efforts coming out quite exactly the same. No worry, the taste buds don't care! Individual customization ensures that the "love" is put into these attractive little tidbits, and they definitely look right at home while adding eye appeal to our sprawling spread of scrumptious goodies.

Blood 'n' Bones

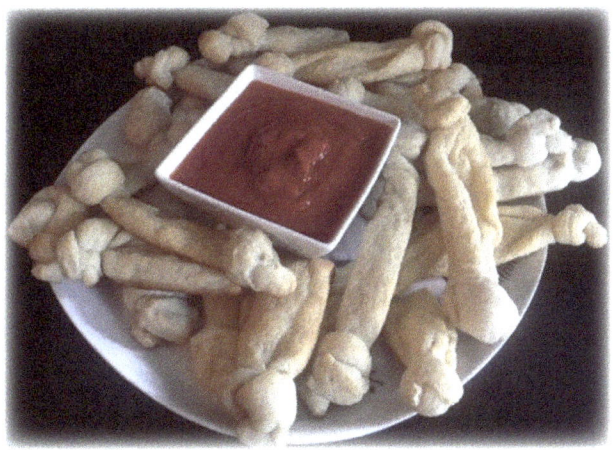

Not exactly sure why this particular platter hits a nerve with me, but it definitely "serves" to put my party mind-set in the right place!

91

## Chips and Crackers

### Skeleton Horrors D'oeuvre Medley

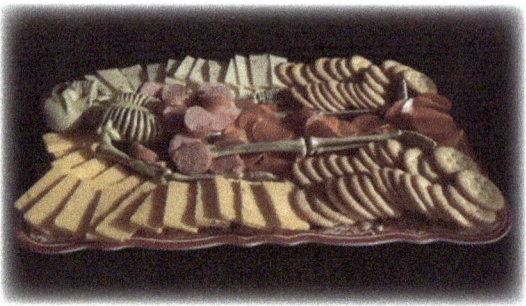

Another spookily splendid display with this skeletons chest cavity pouring out an assortment of fiend friendly favorites.

### Pumpkin Puke

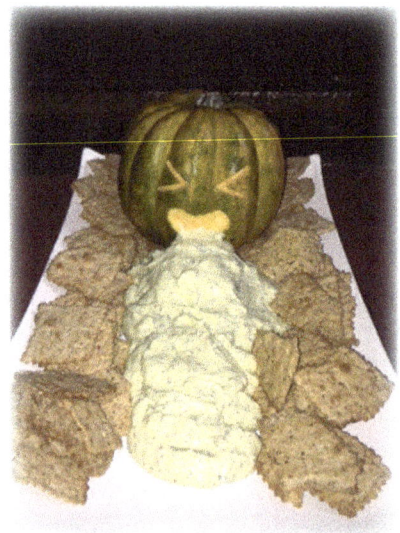

As distasteful a dish as this may appear, if done correctly, the presentation does nothing to dissuade ones taste buds, particularly when suffering from a good case of the munchies.

Salsa Surprise

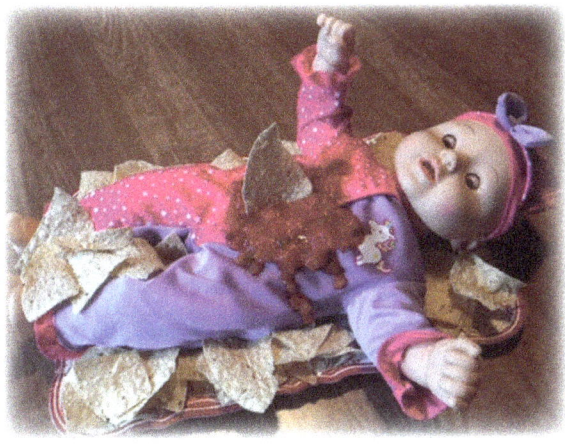

Just plain sick! Who invited the individual responsible for this outrage? Just how maniacal are we allowed to get here anyway?

Healthy Eats

Ghosts in the Pumpkin Patch

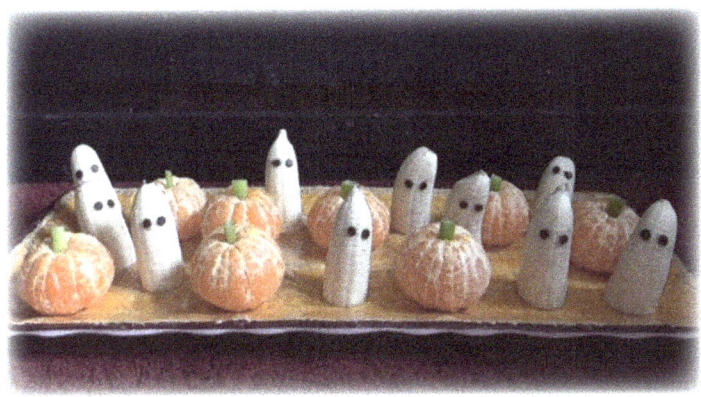

Now that's more like it...friendly little ghosts amongst the pumpkins, perhaps aimed at our more health-conscientious castle dwellers.

## Goblin Grins in the Greens

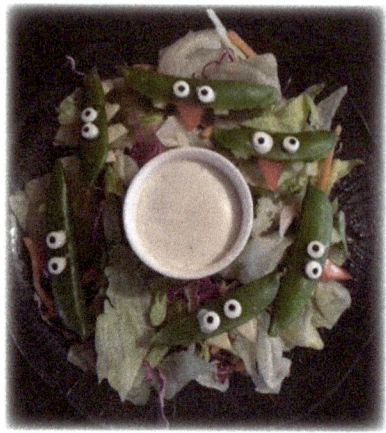

Speaking of healthy, these mini monster mouths are sure to dress up ANY first course. Again, variations on the theme remain endless!

## Deserts

### Spider Cookies

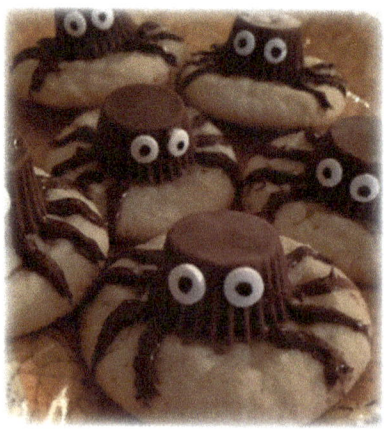

Just TRY not to like these little critters! They're fun to look at and awesomely delicious all at the same time.

## Graveyard Cake

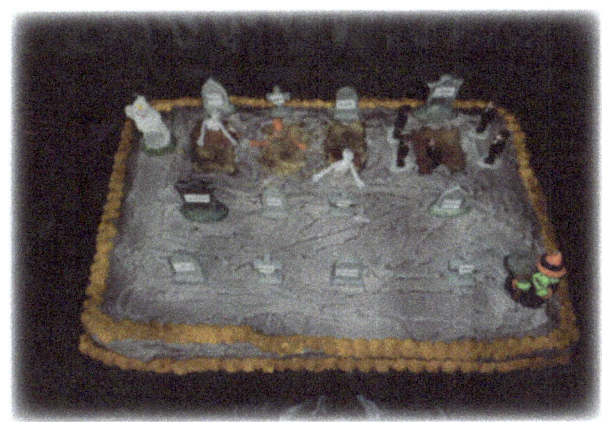

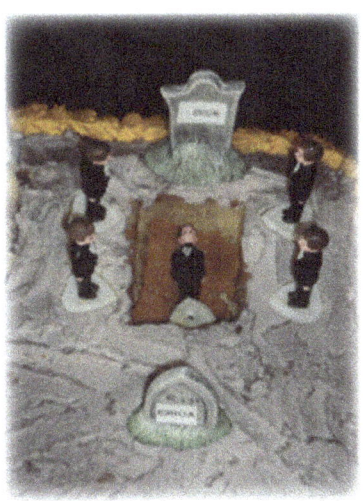

The graveyard cake is a tradition at our annual "All Hallows' Eve" extravaganza. It's a creation offered up by my father-in-law each year, and as you can see, he very much gets into the spirit of the event by customizing the headstones of each cake, labeling them with the names of some of our party "regulars." They certainly get a kick out of his effort . . . not to mention the fact that the cake always tastes great too!

## Kitty Litter

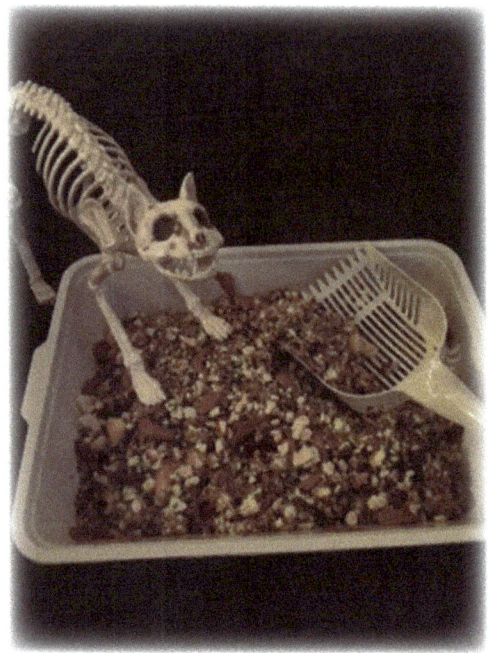

This little creative concoction is appealing on a number of levels. It's both visually stimulating and mentally alarming all at the same time. But perhaps best of all, it is one of the tastiest items Frankenstein has at his feast table. With the topping being made up of any one of an assortment of sweet crumbly offerings, the base maintains a puddinglike element to it. Particularly here, presentation speaks volumes.

## Liquid Embellishment

### Baby Barkeep

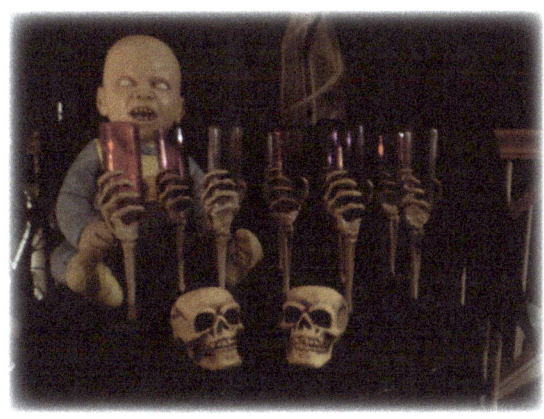

In staying with the theme for the evening, these tall skeleton handheld shot glasses make for the perfect dispensers for a quick drink while our diminutive bartender for the night remains mindful not to overserve.

### Frankenstein's Laboratory

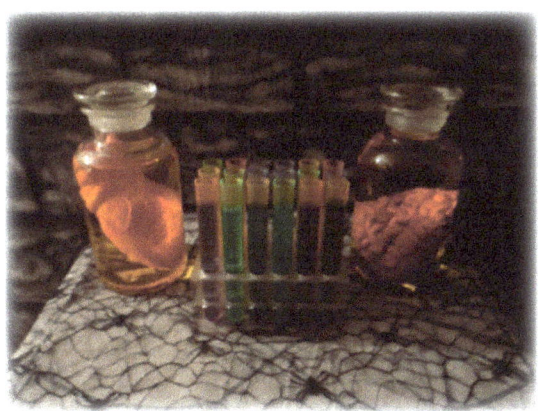

Here we find some select organs preserved in jars serving as the perfect backdrop against which to offer up some sort of test tube contained "elixir"

straight from Dr. Frankenstein's laboratory. For effect, the liquid in the jars is of course tinged with food coloring while the concoction in the test tubes was customized to best suit our guests' personal taste.

Eyeball Punch

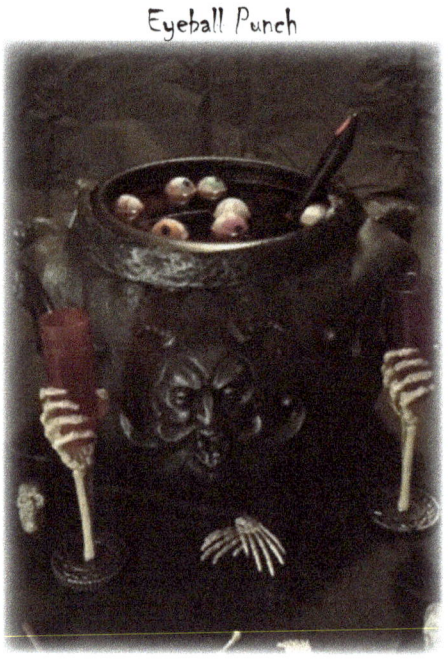

Visually intoxicating, an absolute treat to behold and always mixed to Frankenstein's exact specifications! Again, presentation is EVERYTHING!

Ideas for creatively presenting food to best suit our feast table spread are truly endless whether they be found on the internet and born out of someone else's imagination or the direct result of one of our own acquaintances using the occasion to visit the deepest recesses of their individually deranged minds. No matter where the impetus gets originated, special kudos go out to those who show up offering a mixture of desire and sheer ingenuity as each event has come to pass. We guarantee your friends will rise to the occasion and monstrously deliver the goods as well, especially as your Halloween celebrations become annual tradition.

In addition to whatever culinary contributions end up on your table, be sure to accessorize as you see fit whether it be through improbable oddities discovered along the way . . .

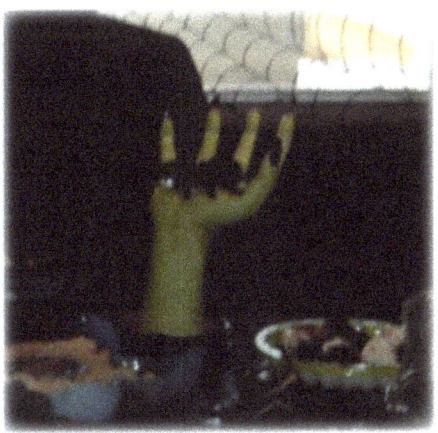

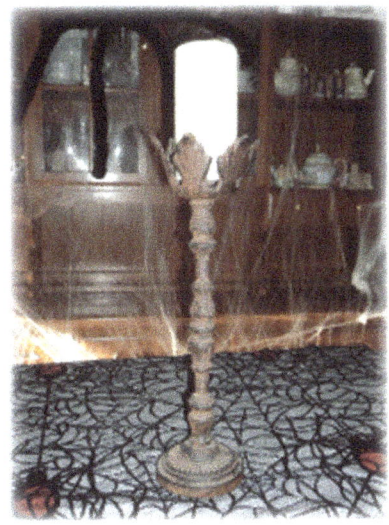

. . . or through items more authentic in nature such as these cast-iron candle holders that have got to weigh three to four pounds each. Once placed on our spiderweb tablecloth, they serve to further blur the line separating fake from real, adding another degree of realism to Frankenstein's feast table.

Of course, Halloween-themed plates and cups are a necessity while other more obscure detail remains up to the host such as a length or two of spidery thread dangling from the ceiling around the feast table or perhaps a skeleton skull chandelier gracing the room, etc.

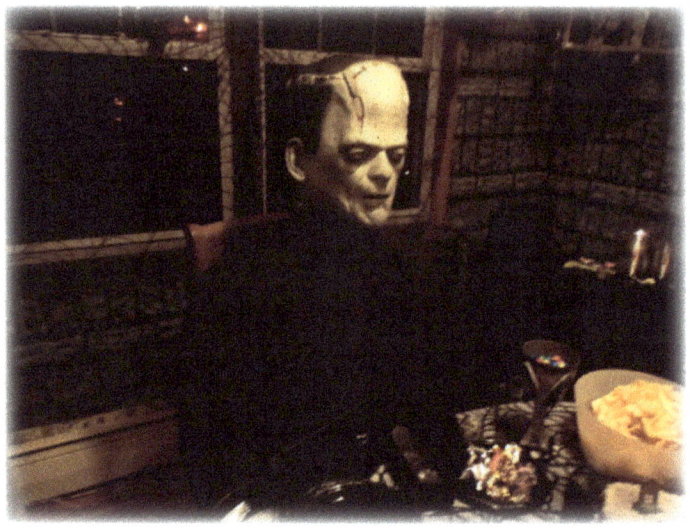

Meanwhile, at OUR party, the "host" remains poised at the head of the table adding more than a suitable measure of ambiance, completing Frankenstein's food setup and rounding out the overall feast room effect.

# Miscellaneous

## Invitations

An invitation to a Halloween masquerade party comes with the added caveat of requiring the invitees to arrive in full costume, which in turn will no doubt be the thoughtful end result of some kind of self-expression. Thus, if you're doing this thing right, your invitations should be sent out with ample time to allow plenty of advance warning, so there's adequate time for your guests to shop for whatever costume is going to make them feel like they <u>belong</u> at your party. This is especially true when people get into creating their own homemade attire, and there are absolutely a number of these individuals found in every crowd! The last thing you want is to create additional stress on your potential partygoers by not allowing sufficient time for people to digest the thought, internally process this odd request, and react accordingly. If you don't, at the very least, the average amount of creativity that would normally be expected to go into a costume choice will be watered down. And in the worst-case scenario, the "shine" will wear off the opportunity to put their best foot forward, and you may lose a portion of your invite list due to "other previous engagements." So be sure to let them get properly motivated and psych themselves up for a good time by giving them plenty of advance notice. Bottom line: <u>send the invitations out early!</u>

Now if you're like us, we have a core group of our "besties" who look forward to attending each and every year, annually competing for best costume accolades and never letting much get in the way of them showing up. It

101

is the individuals on this primary list that we send an initial "feeler" out to ensure the chosen Saturday doesn't adversely affect their ability to attend, etc. This is usually accomplished via e-mail. Only then after we've gained a consensus do we start to put together the actual invitations. But by proceeding cautiously in this manner, we know our core group is IN, and they're already getting prepared!

Still, to ensure that we round out the guest list to a reasonably raucous party number (the more, the merrier), we always include "newbies." This list gets generated from new acquaintances (parents from the kids' school sports teams, fellow employees from work, friends or relatives of the A list, or even from the previous years' B list. Note: You can usually expect half of these people to be "no-shows." They don't know what they're missing). We have found that this list is nearly as essential as the core group. Even if you're seriously into the Halloween scene, very few people get invited to a party of this magnitude when it comes to the level of detail involved within such confined space and time (at least in our case). By introducing new people to the mix, it keeps the party atmosphere fresh. No two parties have ever been quite the same, in part, due to the diversity of our guest list.

With this in mind, you may want to break the invitations into two distinct groups: the first, you expect something from; the second, you simply ask to come. While you may request that everyone attempts to bring some kind of food item with them should they "think of it," you can usually count on your core group to come through with more meaningful delicacies everyone can sink their teeth (and mindsets) into, and that no doubt will look like they actually belong on your dungeon's feast table. Newbies won't fully understand...yet...so don't count on too much from them. Still you can't have too many tasty treats, so don't be bashful about requesting on your formal invitation that people bring something toward the effort. While you're responsible for making sure the essentials are there, you have enough to worry about without filling in all the complimentary munchie requirements, and most of your invitees won't mind rounding out the menu anyway. As a matter of fact, many INSIST! Just remember to hint at themed foods for your event. Some pleasant surprises are bound to show up!

With that said, it's pretty easy to go online these days and download yourself some spooky enough visuals to properly create your own, homemade invitations. And that's probably the best way to go about it from a cost (as well as a customization) standpoint. Our earlier attempts at making invitations were based on just that approach by perhaps using the black silhouette of a haunted house as a central focal point with some extra do-dads (witches, ghosts, pumpkins, etc) here and there for additional pizzazz. But like most other things associated with our annual Halloween bash, the last couple of events we've held were deserving of an upgrade, which we accomplished by taking the same picture we used to create the "covers" for the music CD prizes and made invitations out of them.

The thing about it is that they're actual pictures of real dungeon doors and the inside of an authentic dungeon. Whether you purchase, go the homemade route, or upgrade to something more sensational, they'll get the attention of your guests. We just think that with all the effort that goes into our current party, authentic dungeon pictures capture the imagination much better (not to mention tying in nicely with the party prizes), ratcheting our party theme up another degree by customizing the invite to the specific get-together in question.

Of course, I shouldn't have to mention including the date of the event, address, start time, and perhaps "costume required" or "best costume con-test" sort of standard fair, but if you're planning on having a scavenger hunt, don't forget to tell them that they'll need to bring a flashlight from home right on the invite (while not necessarily telling them why)!

# Fun with Costumes

Over the years, our guests have greatly entertained us by incorporating a wide variety of costume ideas from classic horror garb to creative "statement" costumes related to current events. Truly, we've never had a party come to pass where we weren't highly impressed by a number of efforts put forth by besties and newbies alike. Helping to drive and maintain this level of elaborateness is an ever-present awareness of the prize for best costume... and now, with the entire party soundtrack at stake, it's no wonder! Whether it's the first-place prize, peer pressure, or just an innate desire to let some inner demons escape on a night when they're more apt to blend with their surroundings, our costumed acquaintances certainly help to drive the life of the party and, as such, are worth examining a little closer.

Face painting has become the norm for several of our "frequent flyers" with one married couple showing up at one of our events as nightmarish, macabre clowns while another guy arrived as Gene Simmons from the band "Kiss" (best costume winner). Another year, the same guy dressed up as Little Red Riding Hood, with his wife masked up as the Big Bad Wolf—a simply awesome piece of work. Yet another year, we had a husband dressed as Faith Hill while his wife came as Tim McGraw (naturally when it came to game time, these two were accordingly separated onto appropriate teams with "Tim" joining the guys side and "Faith" rounding out the girls). As a matter of fact, each year we seem to have at least one person who "joins the other team" in the spirit of the party. We appreciate the effort.

From jesters and aliens to vampires and mummies, we've seen a little bit of everything come through our front door at one time or another...all in the spirit of fun. One year, we had "squatters" set up camp on our front lawn prior to ever making an entrance. Another time, I had one of my closest friends show up at the front door dressed as a "nerd" to such an extreme degree that no matter how long I stared at him, I had no clue who he was (he had shaved his well-aged facial hair as part of the getup)! Whatever it is that encourages our guest list to go to the extent they do, we're not exactly sure. I do know that the environment we create greatly adds to their mind-set when deciding what to wear, but somehow I think it's just as much their own true nature, and this occasion simply gives them an outlet to share their inner selves. Whatever the reason, the party is definitely all the better for it!

So of course, as hosts of this annual gathering, we're obliged to not only partake but to help lead the way regarding any infused level of zaniness. For example, while not being as young as I once was (or in the greatest shape), I donned a "Mr. Incredible" outfit for one of our events...much to my wife's delight! My physique was well on display that evening all decked out in a brightly colored muscly body suit. But I've got to tell you...with the mask in place, striking a pose with hands on hips, I felt right at home and was quite the hit!

Another year, I took on more of a "host" look, and although it may sound pretty cliché to say that I dressed up as a gothic vampire that year, the attire came from an exquisite little not-too-far-out-of-the-way costume shop and appeared vividly authentic with the quality of the robe/cape leading the way, a set of fangs in my face, a complimentary handpicked goblet to sip my drink of choice out of and an accent that wouldn't quit.

Then two to three years later, what do I do? Since the cast of characters was expected to be significantly altered on this particular occasion, I came as Mr. Incredible...dressed as a gothic vampire, wearing one costume over the other. It was a free getup, and once again, I was a hit! Silly, huh? You bet. But most had never seen either costume, so when I took off the gothic-vampire attire about halfway through the party claiming that I had had enough and just wanted to be "myself" for the remainder of the night, it was widely received with a chuckle.

The Quick Change—I remember the first time I changed costumes mid-party, I was sure that most of our guests would almost immediately figure out what I was up to. I was wrong! After spending a number of hours in that Mr. Incredible outfit (it made my wife laugh when I tried it on at the costume store, assuring me all along that "it was me"), I slipped into our bedroom somewhere near the height of the party, only to reemerge soon thereafter...as a woman! What I didn't know at the time is that some late arrivals had shown up, and the general populous believed that I was with them!

On top of the perfect timing, my disguise was quite good—a plastic mask (you know the one with the brightly colored makeup plastered on a form-fitting clear plastic face), a shoulder-length blond wig, with my wife's bathrobe completing my ensemble. As it turned out, initially no one but my wife knew it was me! I mean, I was literally walking right up face-to-face with individuals who I had just spent the last three to four hours partying with, and they had absolutely NO CLUE it was me! It was great fun for as long as it lasted. I was informed later (after changing back) that there were still people who didn't understand it was me behind the mask. The point here is that parties are supposed to be fun, and I certainly got more than my fair share for about fifteen minutes by dawning a $2.00 mask, a cheap wig, and my wife's robe from the closet. I knew it was convincing enough, having played around with it in front of family members prior to the party, but I never dreamed I'd have so much fun watching my friends' faces go blank as (without saying a word) I "batted" my eyes and cozied up to one after another of them, putting on a show until I made my exit several minutes later. I've also donned this outfit at subsequent parties, knowing full well that most are aware it's me. Turns out, it's just as much fun knowing the majority are in on the gag (and get to watch) as I totally confuse new invitees.

# Other Uses for the Castle

Once set up, our castle environment is quite the spectacle to behold. Obviously some significant effort goes into putting it all together for the sake of entertaining our friends for one single evening out of the year. So much so, that we've been somewhat hesitant to tear it down on more than one occasion.

As it is, from start to finish, we live in our dungeon-ized home for three to four weeks every year, very rarely attending to the task of breaking it all down and getting everything back up into storage by the following weekend. And why should we? It's the season...and makes for a great conversation piece. Besides, it has a certain "feel" to it.

For weeks, we wake up in our castle, eat meals with "Frank" at the feast table, watch TV in the torture chamber, etc. It's turned into kind of a family tradition, but on top of simply chilling out in our virtual castle, some other opportunities have come to light.

My daughter's birthday happens to fall in the third week of November. Knowing that a lot of kids get a special "sweet sixteen" party thrown for them by their parents (no doubt costing some added cash no matter the venue), we threw Alice and a bunch of her sixteen-year-old girlfriends a costume party! While she had some work to do with the invitations and the creation of her own soundtrack for the event, we were more than all set to rise to the occasion. The place is more than extravagantly decorated, the games are all in place, and on the night of the party, my wife and I (as hosts of the evening) chaperoned in full complementary garb! And did they have fun or what? It was a tremendous hit!

As kids were getting dropped off, the parents' eyes were just as wide in amazement as the invited girls. Each time the front door opened, everything just hit them in the face all at once. One by one, they were welcomed to venture in to get a better look at some of the detail involved with our "castle." You can imagine how it went over. We had one dad come back to pick up his daughter offering us a bottle of wine for showing his kid such a good time, not believing we went to such extremes for our daughter's "sweet 16." Another dad who had dropped off his daughter earlier came back to pick up with his whole family in tow asking for a quick tour to share what he had seen. So the Mom, two additional daughters, and the dad (again) received a full tour. And of course, we love it when our work gets noticed and receives such accolades. (Many who attend agree that the local paper should be here

to take pictures. Some insist I need to write a "Halloween book." Hmm...).
At any rate, it's certainly an impressive creation.

We've even taken the castle on the road (sans the wallpaper)! My wife's parents have a camp on a lake up in Maine, and every year, they have a Halloween event in the middle of the summer, complete with trick or treating for the kids. Over the years, the lakes inhabitants began to adorn their campsites with more and more decoration until finally, the owner was awarding prizes for best setup! Well, say no more! After a little prodding from my kids, we stuffed as much of the "good stuff" into our SUV as we could and headed up to satisfy their itch to enter the contest. Long story short, we came, we set up, we conquered, winning first prize and associated bragging rights for my in-laws for the year. In essence, I guess you can say that we truly have an award-winning approach to conveying the Halloween spirit through our selection of props!

Last, although we haven't followed through with it, we've also considered the notion that we could remove the Halloween accent by taking out all the "scary" stuff and just leave the castle effects—the wall covering, flame pots, weaponry, the thunderstorm, etc. We could create another, more suitable soundtrack to delve us into medieval times and throw a dinner or cocktail party for our closer-knit group of friends. We could add to the entertainment by catering in the food and/or having a wine tasting brought in. Just a thought...

## So What's Next?

We've found that our guests can get so caught up in their virtual castlelike surroundings that some have been known to be a little gullible at times. For example, at one gathering, we had a number of individuals searching for a trap door we told them we had installed explaining that it was going to be used for one of our customized game time competitions later in the evening, and that if they found it, they were not to tell anyone so as not to spoil the surprise. On and off throughout the night, they could be found (in between intermittent bursts of fog) searching the hardwood floors for a latch, seam, or any evidence of this so-called "trap door." All right...maybe we had a little bit TOO much fun that night, but it was proof that we could get them believing that nearly ANYTHING was possible in our mocked-up castle.

By practically demanding that we throw our Halloween party every year, our guests have come to expect us to elevate our game with each iteration relative to past experiences. After delivering several productions, one would think that this additional pressure to produce a worthy enough event would become daunting at best. After all, given a limited amount of living space to work with, once we've filled it with the most impressive props/effects our budget will support, what are we to do? The answer? We continue to think out of the box! Along with keeping a sharp look out for anything new that might catch our eye out on the market, we continue to try to utilize what we already have to our best advantage. So what's next?

Ghostly Presence—Take a look at the following picture. What do you see?

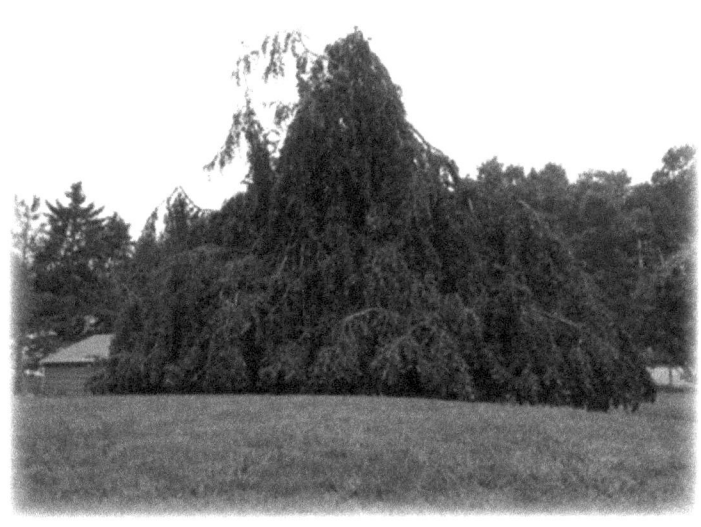

Impressive, huh? This tree sits smack dab in the middle of our backyard and takes up a pretty good chunk of real estate too, measuring approximately thirty feet high and over forty feet across. One might even say it's somewhat of a monster of a tree, eh? But look at the shape! Maybe it's just me, but with very little imagination, I can envision the biggest ghost in the entire neighborhood coming to life before my eyes. Can you see it? I wonder how many king-sized sheets I'd have to sew together to cover this gargantuan, perfectly shaped tree to create the grandest prop ever!

With very little trimming to accommodate, the only trick would be (short of renting a "cherry picker") how to get the supersized ghost costume over the tree? Hmmm...I do own decent sized ladders and gained some relevant experience stringing Christmas lights onto a sizeable tree in the front yard using nothing more than a long pole with a bent wire coat hanger attached to the end, but can it be done? I wouldn't bet against me. It certainly would "WOW" the crowd, and THAT'S what keeps my creativity evolving. I can just envision this thing with just the right amount of light cast upon it from a couple different angles, causing eyes to widen in an attempt to refocus from inside the dungeon windows almost in disbelief at the sheer size of it. I can picture having our scavenger hunt out back with this GIGANTIC ghost overseeing our every move. Awesome!

Arachnid Encounter—It turns out that the repelling spider we created is an excellent source of entertainment for anyone who wants to engage in a little fun. Upon descending down into the party, the wobbling motion the spider exhibits adds to this toy's appeal and has proven to be a favorite among our party revelers. This fact has not gone unnoticed and could, in turn, trigger another creative idea. Why not simulate an entire nest of arachnids, perhaps located directly over the feast table that would all descend downward at the throw of a single switch? It would be simple enough to fabricate, using a similar motor with a single thread running out from the spool eventually tied to a series of several individual strands, all attached to their own respective spiders. Just mount the motor and a few small eye-hooks later...voila! One more fun gadget for the crowd to have at . . . a swarm of spiders dropping down all at once from several spots in the ceiling to investigate our food spread! The fact that it's interactive definitely ramps up the attractiveness of this little event upgrade, and the cost would be negligible!

House of the Damned—Another inexpensive addition to our annual house of horror was discovered while thumbing through some Halloween-related website. While I can't take credit for this one, I found immediate value in the illusion it provides, and it's simple enough to create. It seems appropriate lengths of cardboard can easily be fashioned to very closely resemble boards which can in turn then be attached to the outside of the house over the windows giving the clear impression that the dwelling itself has been condemned! Absolutely LOVE the effect and plan on incorporating this one at future events!

Ghostly Aberration—All right, let's really get the innovation going here. I wonder how much it would cost to take our candy corn-illusion-maker concept and SUPERSIZE it! I mean, if it doesn't "break the bank" to get a decent sized reflector made, I can easily envision cutting a hole in the middle of a card table, mounting the reflector underneath, perhaps leak a little fog action through it and (with or without holding a bona fide séance) create an effect that actually results in a life-sized floating head . . . right before everyone's eyes! Or even better, put it in a closet or set it up in an empty bedroom, presentation remaining key or, depending on the size of the reflector and subsequent illusionary figure, bury it in the ground out in the backyard producing a perfectly ghostly, supersized aberration! Don't laugh! I admit that it sounds a little far-fetched, but I know none of my friends would put it past me. You should see what I've accomplished for some of my OTHER parties.

# Hints for the Host

Work full time? Don't stress! I'm very aware of the time involved with our castle setup and advise you to do what I do—plan accordingly. All right, so maybe I go a little overboard with all that goes into our particular Halloween production, but I spread out the "pain" by starting to hang the wallpaper two full weeks in advance. Then throughout the remaining time leading up to the party, I poke away at the individual setups, meaning I attend to the construction of the major props. Everything has to find its way out of storage, out of a box, and into its temporary location one by one.

On the weekend prior to the event, I finish the wallpaper and begin setting up any of the remaining props in earnest, always cognizant of the time I have left to complete the transformation of our house. The party is always on a Saturday, and I have been known to take the preceding Friday off from work just to cater to any last minute setup needs so my time is as freed up as it can be come party time. And there's always still plenty to do the day of...with breaking out the food, drink, ice, getting into costume, checking the music, lighting...even some of the props have to wait until the last minute to be placed appropriately (i.e., you can't take a shower with a boar's head in the tub or get into the linen closet with a creepy-crawly chick emerging from a static TV in front of the door, etc.). The point here is, give yourself enough time to do whatever has to be accomplished because whatever amount of time remains, you'll need to put on the final touches.

Speaking of your costume, as the host, remember that maneuverability is a must! You need to be a social butterfly, hopping from one group to the next to entertain, messing with the music, offering drinks, organizing games, etc. So your costume should not interfere with your ability to ensure that all is going well at a pace that is most conducive to a good time. At one of the first Halloween bashes we threw, I dressed up as a priest, who happened to have a wrought iron "rod" lodged through his body, entering me up high on the right shoulder, seemingly passing through my torso, and exiting down and across my body reappearing out of my upper left thigh. (I bought the priest outfit and fashioned the rod myself, attaching the two protruding lengths of rod to metal angles mounted on leather straps held in place around my chest and thigh with seamstress's elastic. Appropriately placed holes in the priest's robe allowed for entrance and exit locations while concealing the supporting mechanics.) It wasn't a bad costume, except for one thing...I kept knocking into people, doorframes, chairs—everything. Not to mention that it was an issue just to sit down to get a load off once in a while throughout the evening.

The other thing I'll mention is you want to stay as cool as possible. I know that up here in the northeast part of the country, October is directly linked to the New England fall season, a time of year when the climate cools off to a significant degree. Just don't count on it! In a house full of partyers, as the host, you'll find plenty to keep yourself busy throughout the course of the evening. All this movement, coupled with the heat generated from your party population (not to mention possible stove use to warm up some goodies) even if the windows are all open, you can't rely on a good breeze to be present on the night of your event. So a word to the wise: Dress for comfort! You'll appreciate it when it's time to party.

At the top of the list of associated "don'ts" is...no full rubber masks but also includes minimal layering if at all possible, etc. Shop for your costume accordingly using your best judgment here.

I even make it a point to leave the air conditioners mounted in the windows for just this reason. Whether it's a warm night or it's pouring rain outside (causing you to all but close the windows), they have been much needed on more than one occasion. So be sure to make an effort to keep you, as well as your invited guests comfortable...further promoting a carefree party atmosphere and one less thing to concern yourself over. Everyone will appreciate it!

As the host, when you throw a party of any substance, one thing above all else becomes very apparent—the overall ongoing "mood." This is particularly true when the event is a house party, confined within the walls of someone's residence. Here, the literal ebb and flow of the "life of the party" is consequently magnified throughout the entire evening. When it's a Halloween party, the crowd gathers in costumed wardrobe over the first hour or so. That, coupled with the elaborate decor of the party environment is certainly enough to breathe initial life into the event. As the crowd continues to grow throughout this period of time, the place inevitably becomes more and more raucous as a crescendo of noise and activity starts to take hold. However, as mentioned earlier, when things start to calm down (and they will), it's time for you to throw a switch, altering your attention from welcoming them...to facilitating the party. We always take this opportunity to roll out the first game time activity to get everyone involved with the proceedings. Generally speaking, after the pomp and circumstance of the first of the night's competitions has come to pass, the party is off and running.

Understanding that the music list is designed to crescendo at the height of the party (helping to grow and maintain a level of excitement/fun throughout the event), recognizing the difference between normal social interaction and an actual dip in the entertainment level, we recommend the following to avoid any such lull, perceived or not.

Periodically demonstrate anything that is interactive and be sure to occasionally revisit these playthings for others who weren't present the first time around. Just in passing, be sure to point out any illusionary trickery that may have been overlooked by some of your houseguests. Include other points of interest as well through conversation such as the fact there's vampires blood in the air, etc.

In short, to the best of your ability, fill the night with entertainment! At our parties, we proceed with exactly that in mind by also...breaking out a round of skeleton handheld shot glasses filled with a house favorite for anyone who wishes to partake, wait for unsuspecting prey and drop our spidery friend down into the party for a timely visit, crank the fog machine up, put on a lightning show in the dungeon, point out the 3-D watch-dragons, the ghost candy or motorized spider, push the button on the pirate/skeleton picture, perform a "quick change" of costume—anything to keep the momentum of the party going! And on three separate occasions at some point in the night, we get into another Halloween-themed competition, keeping the entertainment aspect of the evening at the forefront!

With so much happening, the night goes by way too fast. Initially the first couple of parties we held included our closest and dearest friends only. That was great for a start, but we learned to include others as parties came to pass which served to significantly up the entertainment value. In the beginning, our guests generally filtered in over the first half of the event. Now knowing what to expect, within the first thirty to forty-five minutes, everyone who is coming has arrived to squeeze every last drop out of "the life of the party!"

# Cost

All this stuff looks pretty elaborate, doesn't it? It's time we took a look at the bottom line. Our castle contents listed in order of approximate expense:

Homemade (some time investment required)
> Frankenstein (all but the mask)
> Repelling Spider
> Giant Cocoons
> Dungeon Dragons (downloaded)
> Customized Party Soundtrack (pennies/song)
> Dungeon Rock CD Prizes
> Thunderstorm Soundtrack (downloaded)
> Virtual Lightning (mounted on posts in yard)
> Bloody Sheet (Boar's)
> Static TV (behind Creepy Crawling Chick)
> Threaded Ceiling (cobweb effect)

Dollar Store
> Mummy Hands (Oven Mitts)
> Witches Brew/Scavenger Hunt Items
> Plastic Cauldrons
> Prize Medallions

$5 to $10
> Giant Rodent
> Ghost Candy Generator
> Vampire Blood Incense
> Small Gargoyles
> Dungeon Weaponry

3' Skeletons (Raise the Dead)
Dungeon Chains
Headstones
Assorted Spiders

$15 to $25

Fog Juice
Set of Bottled Serums
Large Illuminated Skull
Motorized Wolf Spider
Fireplace Bones
Candelabra
Cat Skeleton
Floating/Talking Heads CD
Flame Pots
Head in Jar
Large Gargoyle
"Pumpkin Head"
Grim Reaper
Giant Skull Face (Eyeballs in the Skull Head)
Haunted Portraits
Medieval Candle Holders
Skull/Candle Chandelier
Fireplace Severed Head
Coffin
Flying Ghoul

$30 to $50

The Sorting Hat
Baby Barkeep
Tentacle Head

Caged Ghoul
Graveyard Fence
Frankenstein (Mask)
Cocooned Corpse
Fog Machine

$60 to $100

Hanging Hooded Ghost
Dungeon Victims (Skeletons)
Graveyard Corpse
Mourning Widow
Spectre
Witch
Roadside Greeter
Grave Digger
Mummy

Over $100

Boars Head—$125 (YIKES...but must have!)
Creepy Crawling Girl—$199 (Ditto)
Castle Wallpaper—$200 ($20/ream, ten reams)

All things considered, this party gets a little pricey, or does it? The total investment easily falls in the neighborhood of a couple thousand dollars, but remember...this stuff was accumulated over a several year period. I look at it like this: How much do I spend on any regular old party? I mean, when we put together say...a birthday party for one of the kids, there's the cake/food, drink, decorations, presents, and should you make it an "event" at the local roller rink, laser tag facility, etc., we up the ante a significant amount. Maybe we rent a "bouncy room" to set up in the backyard for the day, whatever. Certainly a few hundred dollars comes to pass with most special occasions, and we're already financing these types of events on an ongoing basis. So what's the big deal in investing a little cash toward an event like THIS one, especially for all your friends who will truly appreciate it?

While it's true that to pull off an initial party of any substance it takes a little "front" money, after that it turns into just a regular party expense and before you know it, you're the guy throwing the annual bash that all your friends talk about until the next one comes around!

So make a plan...and not necessarily for this year. Plan it for next year instead and give yourself some time to squirrel away a little cash. Set aside some of the tax refund, start a party "pool" and throw ten or twenty bucks in it every now and again. And stay alert! You get the best bargains in the "off season," so don't wait until Halloween is upon you to go out shopping. And remember to inquire about the floor displays, especially the bigger ticket items since you can usually wrangle a discount out of the proprietor (be sure to examine thoroughly for scratches/dents. It inevitably ups the amount of the discount). If you're into parties and have friends like yourself who are just looking for a reason to get stupid, Halloween is the perfect vehicle to satisfy all!

# Final Word

Perhaps Ben Franklin was right, maybe "we grow old because we stop playing." But even if that's so, we're very pleased to announce that the aging process will have to wait because personally, we're just not ready to stop playing... with my OCD apparently playing a role toward that end.

Still we look back at the several Halloween events we've held over the years and wonder what our friends must think of us, going to the extent we do for the sake of showing them a good time. Certainly they've at least considered the possibility that we're a bit "left of center." But here's what I think, and it's simple. I heard someone once say that if you're not busy living, you're busy dying. Suffice it to say, I think you know which side of the coin we remain on.

With that in mind, while our aim is to share, as well as entertain, we hope you've enjoyed (and more importantly got something useful out of) the contents of this book. In the end, if we've played even a small part in spreading a little happiness, it would please us no end.

Finally, we'd like to applaud each and every last one of our guests over the years for attending our annual Halloween get-togethers. Without you, this book would not have been possible, so thank you all for helping to drive the "life of the party!"

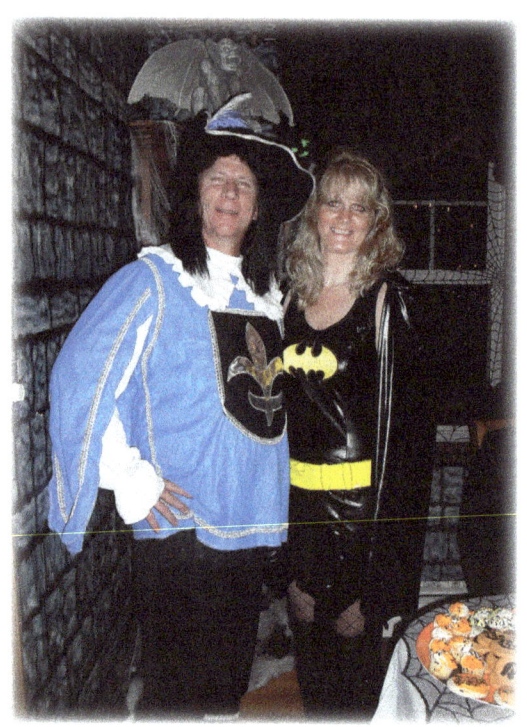

Happy Halloween
From Sue and Dick

# About the Author

Dick Durland is the self-proclaimed "king of the theme party," possessing an extensive collection of extraordinary artifacts he keeps stored away on his property accumulated over the years from hosting a wide variety of themed events. Everything from home-crafted casino games to supersized graduation caps fill his residence—a house that (at least for one day) found itself enveloped in an enormous black belt in celebration of one of his son's achievements. Totem poles and palm trees live in his backyard, Halloween in the attic, a New Year's Eve "ball drop" in the shed, and where most people house their automobile in their garage...in his, you'll find a fully functioning volcano. By day, Dick is a degreed engineer who lives with his wife, Susan, and three children. After hours, he remains a party die-hard.

www.ingramcontent.com/pod-product-compliance
Lightning Source LLC
Chambersburg PA
CBHW040108180526
45172CB00009B/1270